Mexican-American Schoolchildren: A Neo-Piagetian Analysis

Edward A. DeAvila
Barbara Havassy
with Juan Pascual-Leone

Georgetown University Press, Washington, D.C. 20057

Library of Congress Cataloging in Publication Data

DeAvila, Edward A.   1937-
' Mexican-American schoolchildren.

    Bibliography: p.
    1. Cognition (Child psychology) 2. Mexican American
children. 3. Piaget, Jean, 1896-   I. Havassy, Bar-
bara, 1942-   joint author.   II. Pascual-Leone,
Juan, joint author.   III. Title.
BF723.C5D39   155.4'13   76-11847
ISBN 0-87840-164-4

International Standard Book Number: 0-87840-164-4

formerly
136.613
D 349

ACKNOWLEDGMENT

This short book may well have never been written were it not for the very real help and guidance of my friend and teacher, Juan Pascual-Leone. Not only have we used his Figural Intersections and Water-Level tests, but the very underpinnings of the entire approach are based on the conceptions provided in much of his earlier work. We thus owe a profound debt for both the practical and theoretical guidance.

In long hours of discussion we reviewed not only the purposes of present research, but also the assumptions and processes underlying the very nature of psychological measurement. We could not have proceeded were it not for these discussions. It is through this type of analysis that Juan Pascual's model allows development of the kind of procedures embodied and described in the following research.

While the theoretical model used follows from basic unpublished research conducted by Juan Pascual-Leone, the practical application and translation from the theory to reality is our own and we take full responsibility for our errors. If this research has any ultimate effect in altering current egregious testing policies, then not only will we owe thanks to Juan Pascual-Leone, but so will the children who are now being badgered and bullied and simply cheated by current approaches.

We would also like to thank Joseph R. Ulibarri for his faith in what we set out to do and for providing financial support through the Multilingual Assessment Program, Stockton, California. We would also like to thank several members of the Multilingual Assessment staff who worked long hours, often without knowing toward what end. Thus, the authors would personally like to acknowledge the contributions of Veronica Hooker, who coordinated much of the data gathering; Bobby Santiago and Marsha McRay, who assisted in data collection in New Mexico; Zack Bernal, who collected data in Colorado; Regio Rios, who served as troubleshooter; and Marvin Hanley, who ran what seemed like an endless number of statistical programs through the computer.

CONTENTS

0

INTRODUCTION

In the early 20th century Alfred Binet (1909:13) said:

> . . . some recent philosophers appear to have given their
> moral support to the deplorable verdict that the intelligence
> of an individual is a fixed quantity . . . We must protest and
> act against this brutal pessimism . . . A child's mind is like
> a field for which an expert farmer has advised a change in
> the method of cultivating, with the result that in place of
> desert land, we now have a harvest. It is in this particular
> sense, the one which is significant, that we say that the in-
> telligence of children may be increased. One increases that
> which constitutes the intelligence of a school child, namely,
> the capacity to learn, to improve with instruction . . .

The importance of Binet's remarks to modern psychological and educational thought is easily recognized, especially with regard to current
controversies surrounding the relation of race or ethnicity to IQ and
the IQ testing of American minority children. It is not necessary to
retrace here the history of the nature-nurture debates, from which
the current battles over the IQ testing of minority children arise. It
is sufficient to say that a great many children in this country, a dis-
proportionate number of whom are of ethnic or racial minorities, are
being placed in classes for the mentally retarded on the basis of IQ
test scores. These tests are based on a concept of intelligence whose
validity has been and still is questioned on philosophical, psychological,
and educational grounds, as are the tests themselves.

The following research represents an attempt to explore empirically
the Piagetian approach to the measurement of cognitive development in
Mexican-American and Anglo-American children in the southwest

1

United States. As will be seen, a rather diverse approach has been taken. While the approach is different, it nevertheless represents a long history of inquiry, the fruits of which we are only beginning to realize.

As early as 1932, George I. Sanchez admonished educators to consider more fully the dangers associated with testing Mexican-American children by means of then available standardized group instruments. Since then little has changed with respect to the availability of less biased instrumentation. To a great extent this is because currently available standardized tests of intelligence have been developed according to the same pragmatic/empirically based psychometric procedures as were used in the early days of American test development-- procedures which do not include Mexican-American content in the construction of test items or Mexican-American subjects in the norming process. During the past few years, however, there has been an increasing concern over the appropriateness of the IQ model, psychometric procedures, and whether the IQ score produced by standardized tests reflects reality with respect to characterizing the intellectual development of the Spanish-language minority child. Our concern with accurate assessment of the intellectual development of a child has brought us to consider an alternative assessment model which builds upon the work of Jean Piaget.

The value of the Piagetian approach with respect to Mexican-American children, above and beyond theoretical arguments, is the consistency of children's performance across diverse linguistic and cultural settings. In a review of Piaget's work, Brown (1965) has indicated that while the Piagetian approach may not be totally free of cultural impact, 'on the whole it is nearer the culture-free pole.' Brown cites the work of Wallach (1963) who, in summarizing a large number of studies conducted in North America and Europe, found that while there are slight shifts in age of acquisition, the same sequential order of acquisition of different conservation tasks is found regardless of location. It is exactly this similarity of sequence across cultural settings that makes the work of Piaget extremely relevant to Mexican-American children. In this context Goodnow (1963), using conservation of space, weight, and volume, tested European and Chinese children in Hong Kong and found no difference in acquisition regardless of level of schooling. A similar conclusion was reached by Merselstein (1968) with Blacks not attending school and Anglos who were attending.

Although not a great deal of research has dealt with the reconciliation of the traditional psychometric approach and the Piagetian procedures, the theoretical and practical value of such a reconciliation has been implied (see Elkind 1971; Phillips 1969). On the theoretical side, it would be valuable to show high indices of validity and reliability across Piagetian tasks and to demonstrate the feasibility of the creation of a developmentally based test of intellectual development that is psychometrically viable. This demonstration would lend support to a nonstatic or environmentalist interpretation of intelligence (see Hunt 1961), the position represented by the words of Binet (1909). On the practical side, such a demonstration would lead toward the development of tests of intelligence which are less culturally biased. One manner of attempting reconciliation would be to take Piagetian items and procedures and to standardize them according to psychometric theory.

In attempting to apply psychometric technique and method to Piagetian content and procedures, it is necessary first to note that Piaget characterizes intellectual development by the extent of internal versus external control of functioning at any given stage of development. In summarizing her work with respect to culture, Goodnow (1963) states that 'the most striking result is the very real and close similarity in performance among boys of different nationality and education' (cited in Brown 1965:235). Test procedures must distinguish between external or environmental variables such as education and social background, and internal or developmental variables. This distinction gives rise to the determination of a subject's intellectual development as a two-step process.

The first step in the process would be the removal or control of the effects of external-environmental variables which may reflect diverse experiential backgrounds, before testing the child. The second step involves the determination of the extent of the internal control through the use of tasks which vary in the degree of control required to produce a correct response.

One way of providing for the control of external variables is through the use of an 'experimental repertoire control' (ERC) procedure. The ERC procedure allows external-environmental differences between subjects to be minimized through pretraining procedures. The procedure has been developed and tested by Pascual-Leone and Smith (1968), Pascual-Leone (1970), and De Avila (1971). It was used by Pascual-Leone (1970) in conjunction with a variety of Piagetian tasks and the Witkin (1962) measures of field dependence-independence in a factor analytic study of cognitive development and cognitive style.

An essential feature of Pascual-Leone's procedure is that prior learning (external-environmental variables) is controlled through pretraining (see Pascual-Leone and Smith 1969). Using prior learning as a control, Pascual-Leone and Smith (1969) have found highly stable results across a number of Piagetian tasks. In another study, with upper-middle-class Canadian children, De Avila (1971) found that when the background of subjects was controlled through use of experimental control tasks, low correlations were found between a standardized intelligence test (Otis-Lennon) and a number of Piagetian tasks developed by De Avila (1971) and Pascual-Leone (1970), while the intercorrelations of the Piagetian tasks were all high (r = . 600).

Such results provide support for the argument that the IQ measure may be highly related to the external variables such as educational and social background, and suggests that when these factors are controlled through pretraining, the correlation between IQ and performance on intellectual tasks is lowered. These findings are of importance because they provide theoretical as well as practical information, particularly with respect to recent controversy concerning the testing of minority children.

A frequently mentioned objection to the use of Piagetian tasks is that they require individual administration, while educational situations usually require group testing because of the large number of subjects involved relative to the manpower available. However, it has been demonstrated that the administration of Piagetian tasks can be adapted to group testing. Dodwell (1961) and Harker (1960) have shown that the child's conception of number can be tested in a group setting, and De Avila and Phyphers (1968), and De Avila, Struthers, and Randall (1969) have measured several conservation tasks along with spatial perspective problems in group situations. De Avila et al. (1969) found adequate reliabilities (r = . 90) for conservation of substance and egocentricity, further suggesting the possibility of using Piagetian-based group measures to evaluate the developmental-psychometric properties of tests which are applicable across a broad range of development in diverse educational and cultural settings. Similarly, Pascual-Leone and Smith (1969) and Pascual-Leone and Parkinson (1969) have adapted a number of Piagetian and neo-Piagetian tasks to group settings with a high degree of success.

The consistency of results on Piagetian tasks across diverse groups of children, and the work of Pascual-Leone and De Avila, may be contrasted with the work of Jensen (1971, 1972), who has attempted to account for IQ differences obtained on standardized IQ tests between Anglo-American and minority-American children by advancing a theory that there are qualitative genetic differences in the intelligence of minority-American and Anglo-American children. These qualitative differences are alleged to account for the difference in quantitative scores on standardized tests of intelligence and suggest inherent differences in ultimate intellectual capacity. Jensen sees a dichotomy in intellectual behavior which rests on distinctions between what he calls Level I abilities, which characterize minority children, and Level II abilities, which describe the intellectual functioning of the Anglo-American child. To quote:

Level I involves simple learning and association, the registering, retention, and retrieval of inputs. It involves very little or no mental manipulation of the input. Level I can be thought of mainly as rote learning and memory. Level II, on the other hand, implies mental manipulation, the ability to deal with complexity, information processing, and the active relating and comparing of present inputs with stored past inputs. It involves the imposing of cognitive structures upon sensory inputs. Level II uses the g factor of intelligence, particularly fluid intelligence. Level I is best measured by memory span for digits, serial rote learning, and trial-and-error selective learning. Level II is best measured by test of fluid intelligence such as Raven's Progressive Matrices and Cattells' Culture Fair Tests of g.

Ramirez (1972) has postulated the presence of an ethnic-individual difference variable to account for IQ differences. Using Witkin's (1962) construct of field independence-field dependence, Ramirez has characterized Mexican-American children as field dependent in contrast to Anglo-American children who are described as field independent.

Differences in field sensitivity, according to Ramirez's position, stem from cultural differences in socialization practices. Anglo-American families, according to Ramirez, encourage the assertion of the individual identities of their members (i.e. 'individualism'), whereas the Mexican-American child develops in a culture which encourages family or group identity. Based on his own research and on the earlier work of Lesser, Fifer, and Clark (1965), Ramirez (1972) has drawn the conclusion that:

> Field sensitive Mexican-Americans do better on verbal tasks of intelligence tests, learn better when the material has human content and is characterized by fantasy and humor, perform better when authority figures express confidence in their ability; and, conversely, their performance is depressed when authority figures express doubt in them.
>
> Field independent Anglo-Americans do better on visual-motor tasks (i.e. putting parts together to make a whole or extracting parts from a whole) of intelligence tests, learn better when material is abstract, impersonal, and tied to reality. Their performance is not significantly affected by the opinion of authority figures.

According to the positions taken by both Ramirez and Jensen, one would expect to find performance differences between Anglo- and Mexican-American children on diverse tests of intellectual behavior, for radically different reasons, however. Both positions have in common the notion that the apparent IQ differences can best be understood through analyses which stress dichotomous (genetic-cultural) differences between groups without regard for the overlap between them. In stressing the differences between Anglo- and Mexican-Americans, both writers have thus far not addressed themselves to the overlap of the two groups which is present in their own data. It appears that a major portion of this overlap may be attributed to sex differences in their data.

While the Jensen and Ramirez positions employ very different causal explanations, functionally speaking their arguments run the risk of being reduced to the same position regarding the educational approach to be taken with Mexican-American children. To argue that Mexican-American children are field sensitive and consequently not receptive to learning abstract, problem-solving strategies is superficially no different, at the practical level, than to argue that the intellectual capabilities of Mexican-Americans are limited to Level I type tasks because of genetic endowment. Both arguments would suggest curriculum for Mexican-American students which eliminates or minimizes tasks requiring the abstract manipulation of impersonal data.

The results of a recent study by Saarni (1973) may well clarify the field-dependence position of Ramirez. Using Piagetian tasks and Witkin's rod and frame task. Saarni (1973) found that Piagetian developmental level, as ascertained by performance on Piagetian tasks, significantly predicted problem-solving performance, whereas level of field independence did not explain individual differences within or across developmental levels. Nevertheless, there were sex differences on the Witkin rod and frame measure. Females at the highest level of cognitive functioning were more field dependent than less able females. Saarni (1973) suggests sociocultural factors influencing rod and frame performance to explain this result.

Such an explanation may be equally applied to the case of Mexican-American children. Thus, while Mexican-American children may, in fact, be more field dependent than Anglo-American children, as hypothesized by Ramirez, this may not necessarily preclude their functioning at the highest cognitive levels, as did the field dependent females in Saarni's (1973) study.

Given these considerations, the present position is one which, on one hand, builds upon an integration of psychometric and Piagetian theory, and on the other, suggests that IQ tests measure a number of attributes over and above intellectual behavior which, to some extent, can be controlled through the pretraining procedures described.

Encouraged by the earlier unpublished extensive results of Pascual-Leone, Parkinson, and De Avila, as well as by the results of the administration of several group Piagetian instruments with a small number of Spanish-background children of low socioeconomic status, the following research represents an attempt to test the approach more fully with a larger sample of Spanish-background children of varied socioeconomic positions.

The research to be described has five basic purposes. The first is to examine the psychometric properties of the several Piagetian-derived measures which were translated into a paper-and-pencil format. The second is to test the developmental properties of these measures within a sample of Mexican-American children of varying socioeconomic status in different areas of the southwestern United States. The third purpose is to examine the relation between developmental level as assessed by these Piagetian-derived procedures and IQ as assessed by standardized approaches across different language, cultural, and SES groups. A fourth purpose is to examine the extent of field independence as measured by Pascual-Leone's Water Level Task (WLT). The fifth major purpose is to compare site and sex differences in performance on neo-Piagetian and standardized achievement and intelligence tests.

The following study is a field study carried out at four different locations: California, New Mexico, Texas, and Colorado. These sites were established through the cooperation of the federal government with the governments of the four states. The state governments selected the actual locations within the states and the site personnel were determined by the internal workings of these governments. The amount, type, and quality of data at each site were limited by personnel at each site. The site personnel were trained in the administration of Piagetian measures by De Avila. The selection of the standardized tests and the training for their administration were site internal matters and were received by the authors as an accomplished fact. With this in mind then, it may be said that the following research reaps the benefits of, and also suffers from the shortcomings of, non-experimental research conducted in natural settings.

CHAPTER 1

METHOD

1.1 Subjects. The sample participating in this study numbered 1,256 boys and girls, in grades one through six, from California, Colorado, New Mexico, and Texas. Their ages range from 6 years, 4 months to 14 years, 8 months. The sample is predominantly Spanish-surnamed. The specific distribution of the sample by site, sex, and age may be found in Table 1.

TABLE 1. Sample description.

Site location	Age and sex groups (age designated by years and months)												Site totals		Percent Spanish surnames per site
	--7.6		7.7-8.6		8.7-9.6		9.7-10.6		10.7-11.6		11.7+				
	M	F	M	F	M	F	M	F	M	F	M	F	M	F	
New Mexico: Albuquerque	40	38	23	32	38	38	44	43	37	38	41	43	223	232	75
	78		55		76		87		75		84		455		
Colorado: San Luis Valley	33	31	17	15	14	10	11	11	16	10	28	31	119	108	97
	64		32		24		22		26		59		227		
Texas: Pharr-San Juan Alamo	18	20	14	14	20	28	25	22	23	18	45	42	145	144	95
	38		28		48		47		41		87		289		
California: Watsonville	24	27	28	18	25	18	24	28	19	21	25	28	145	140	98
	51		46		43		52		40		53		285		
Sex-group totals	115	116	82	79	97	94	104	104	95	87	139	144	632	624	
Age-group totals	231		161		191		208		182		283		1256		

As may be seen by examining Table 1, the number of children at each site differs and each site has different age, sex, and grade distributions. In addition to these differences, the sites vary with respect to certain demographic variables. To the extent that socioeconomic status and school achievement are highly related, the collection of demographic data provides the opportunity to compare performance data to demographic data. Unfortunately, however, it was not possible to obtain quantifiable demographic data which could be used to examine the relation of these variables to performance on both Piagetian and

8

standardized instruments within different sub-samples. In a later section an attempt will be made to describe some of the site differences in
order to provide the reader with at least a basic understanding of the
geographic areas.

1.2 Procedure. The tests administered to subjects consisted of
two types: developmental measures administered to all subjects at
every site, and standardized achievement and IQ tests administered
on a site specific basis. The former group consists of four neo-
Piagetian measures. The first of these, the Cartoon Conservation
Scales (CCS), was developed by De Avila (see De Avila 1971, 1972;
De Avila and Phyphers 1968; De Avila, Struthers, and Randall 1969),
and involves the concepts of conservation of number, substance,
length, weight, and the concept of egocentricity. The second is the
Water Level Task (WLT) developed by Pascual-Leone (1966, 1970)
and used by De Avila (1972). This test measures the conservation of
the horizontality of water and has been shown to be correlated to field
dependence as measured by Watkins' rod and frame task. The third
test is the Figural Intersection Task (FIT), which is a figural analogue
of Piaget's 'intersection of classes' (1932). Pascual-Leone and Parkinson (1969) have collected extensive data showing that the FIT has a
high correlation with the WLT and with a number of other Piagetian-
based measures of cognitive development. The fourth test used was
a short-term memory task. the Serial Task (ST), developed by De
Avila (1971), which is similar to digit span in the WISC.
The standardized tests administered vary from site to site. They
include the Stanford Early School Achievement Test (SESAT), the Otis-
Lennon Mental Ability Test, the Comprehensive Test of Basic Skills
(CTBS), the Inter-American Series, the California Short Form Test of
Mental Maturity (CTMM), and the Peabody Picture Vocabulary Test
(PPVT). The specific forms and levels of each test administered at
each site may be found in Table 2.
In the following section each of the four neo-Piagetian tests is
described in detail.

1.3 Measures

1.3.1 Cartoon Conservation Scales (CCS). Several measures of
Piaget's conservation tasks were assessed by means of the cartoon
format developed by De Avila et al. (1968a, 1968b, 1969). In De Avila's
procedure, three cartoon frames are presented in which two children
discuss a Piagetian task. In the first frame an equality is established
between two objects according to the dimension being studied (i. e.
number, length, substance, etc.). In the second frame an identity
transformation takes place and a question of equivalence is asked.

TABLE 2. Standardized tests administered at four southwestern sites.

Site 1, New Mexico:
  Stanford Early School Achievement Test (SESAT)
    Level II, Grade 1
  Otis-Lennon Mental Ability Test
    Elementary I Level, Form J, Grades 2 and 3
    Elementary II Level, Form J, Grades 4, 5, and 6
    Primary II Level, Form J, Grade 1
  Comprehensive Test of Basic Skills (CTBS)
    Level I, Form Q, Grades 2 and 3
    Level II, Form Q, Grades 5 and 6
    Level II, Form R, Grade 4

Site 2, Colorado:
  California Short Form Test of Mental Maturity (CTMM)
    Level I, 1963, S Form, Grades 1 and 2
    Level Ih, 1963, S Form, Grade 3
    Level II, 1963, S Form, Grades 4, 5, and 6
  California Achievement Test
    Level I, Grade 1
    Level II, Form A, Grades 2 and 3
    Level III, Form A, Grades 4, 5, and 6

Site 3, Texas:
  Inter-American Tests (New Series)
  Test of Reading
    Level I, Form D (English) R-1-DE, Grade 1
    Level II, Form D (English) R-2-DE, Grades 2 and 3
    Level III, Form D (English) R-3-DE, Grades 4, 5, and 6
  Test of General Ability
    Level III, Form C (English) GA-3-CE, Grades 4, 5, and 6

Site 4, California:
  Peabody Picture Vocabulary Test (Spanish translation)
    Form A, Grades 1-6

On the right side of the panel three possible answers are presented. The three alternatives which show the characters responding to the question are randomly ordered to avoid the possible effects of position set or acquiescence.

The CCS consists of thirty cartoon panels: six examples for each of five tasks. The panels are presented to the subjects and the story line read and elaborated upon in order to facilitate understanding of the question. The subjects' task is simply to mark the one (alternative) 'that makes the story true'. Incorrect alternatives were based on those most popularly given by children of similar ages and backgrounds.

1.3.1.1 Number. Conservation of number is measured by showing objects on a table. The dialogue is as follows: Frame 1: 'How many blocks are there?' 'Are there as many on each side now?' There are three possible responses from which the child chooses his answer, two inequalities and one equality. His task is to put an X on the picture 'that makes the story true'.

1.3.1.2 Length. Conservation of length requires that a subject recognize that no matter where a given object is placed, its length does not change. An example from the CCS involves a boy and girl sweeping the sidewalk. The dialogue in Frame 1 is: 'This sure is a big broom.' 'It isn't bigger than mine.' Frame 2: They compare. 'See!' 'Yeah. They're both just as long.' Frame 3: Placed at approximately right angles to each other. 'Let's put them down this way.' 'Are they both just as long now?' The response order is: 'This one is longer' (points to broom on the right). 'This one is longer' (broom on left). 'They are both the same' (points to both brooms).

1.3.1.3 Substance. Conservation of substance is measured in the cartoons where the following type of dialogue takes place.
Frame 1: 'See the two clay balls.' 'They both have just the same amount of clay.' Frame 2: 'What if I roll this one into a flat pancake shape?' Frame 3: 'Does one of them have more than the other one now?' The responses are: (girl points to both) 'They are both the same' (points to ball). 'This one has more' (points to pancake). 'This one has more.'

1.3.1.4 Egocentricity. In this measure, the subject is asked to picture how a setting would look from a perspective other than the one from which he is looking. One illustration from the CCS uses the situation of taking a picture of a toy barn, silo, and tractor. The following dialogue takes place. Frame 1: 'Take a picture of my farm.' 'O.K.' Frame 2: 'I'll take the picture from here.' (View opposite that of the person who 'owns' the farm.) Frame 3: 'What will the picture look like?' The response frames show the picture taker's viewpoint, the owner's viewpoint, and a side view, each with the caption, 'It will look like this.'

1.3.1.5 Weight. Conservation of weight is illustrated in the CCS by using two children balancing on a seesaw. In the first frame, they are shown from a distance and one child says, 'Hey, this seesaw is fun. We can go up and down.' Frame 2: 'Let's see what happens when we stop.' In the third frame, the two children are shown in a balanced horizontal position and one child asks, 'What will happen if I lie down?' The three alternative answers show the seesaw in several positions, with the child who asked the question in a lying down position. It should be noted that the position of the child who is lying down is depicted in such a way as to indicate no change in the distance between himself and the fulcrum (seesaw center post) so as not to alter the leverage relationships.

1.3.2 Water Level Task (WLT). The conservation of the horizontality of water measure utilized here was introduced by Pascual-Leone (1966, 1970) as a standardized quantifiable version of the Piagetian task (Piaget and Inhelder 1956). A more complete description of the relative parameters of this task and its relation to Witkin's field dependency construct may be found in the semantic-pragmatic analysis by Pascual-Leone (1970).

In the present study, a special version of Pascual-Leone's group test was used. Subjects were presented with individual booklets which contained five horizontal or vertical two-dimensional bottles, eight two-dimensional tilted bottles, and four three-dimensional bottles. The subject was asked to draw a line where the top of the water would be if the bottle were half full and then to place an X in the part that contained the water.

1.3.3 Figural Insersection Test (FIT). The Figural Intersection Test is a group administered paper-and-pencil test in which subjects are required to place a dot in the intersecting space of a varying number of geometric figures. It was developed by Pascual-Leone and constitutes a figural analogue of Piaget's 'Intersection of Classes' (1952). The types of overlapping figures utilized in this test were originally devised for another purpose. In a series of unpublished studies, Pascual-Leone has shown the test to have a high degree of internal consistency (split-half reliability = .89), as well as to be significantly related to tests of similar logical structure (Pascual-Leone and Smith 1969; Pascual-Leone and Parkinson 1969).

1.3.4 Serial Task (ST). The Serial Task (De Avila 1971) is a short-term memory task which is individually administered in two phases. First, subjects are preexposed to the stimulus materials used in a subsequent testing phase. In the preexposure or pretraining phase, each subject is shown a series of ten different 35 mm.

color slide pictures depicting a donkey, house, airplane, etc. Subjects sit facing a screen situated on a wall six feet away. Stimuli are presented by means of a Kodak 650 Carousel slide projector and subjects are asked to give its name and color (e. g. 'a yellow hat'). Following this initial introductory phase, and after the subject is able to correctly identify each figure ten times when presented in rapid random succession, the testing phase is begun.

The test phase is conducted in a 'free recall' manner (Adams 1967) where, without any prior knowledge of the length of a list, the subject is asked to reproduce the list, ignoring the order in which the individual items are presented. Subjects are shown a series of individually presented figures terminated by a blank slide, and are asked to tell the experimenter what they saw. The exposure time for each individual slide was .750 msec.

These four tests were given in either English or Spanish, according to the needs of the child as determined by the test administrators. In order to avoid sequence effects, all tests were randomly administered to all subjects within a one-week period. Test administrators were all trained together and consisted of approximately an equal number of males and females. With the exception of one female at the New Mexico site who spoke only English, all test administrators were bilingual and residents of the local test area. Standardized testing was conducted according to the test manual instructions. The only exception to this was in California, where a Spanish translation of the Peabody was used. All other standardized testing was done in English.

CHAPTER 2

RESULTS OF TOTAL SAMPLE DATA

The presentation of results in this chapter is limited to those data on the neo-Piagetian tests which relate to psychometric and developmental issues. The discussion focuses on the psychometric properties of the neo-Piagetian tests as a whole, as well as on the developmental properties of these tests across different age groups. The results obtained at each site are presented on a site-by-site basis in Chapter 3. These presentation data include performance data on the neo-Piagetian tests as well as on the standardized ones. Chapter 4 presents the results of attempts to compare the sites in terms of their performance.

There are two basic relationships which must be considered in any integration of the psychometric and developmental approaches to test analysis and construction. The first concerns the relation of many subjects to an item or question, whereas the second is based on the relation of one subject to many items. In other words, in the traditional psychometric test construction and analysis approach the subjects are varied and the item is held constant whereas in contrast, in the developmental approach that Piaget has taken, items are varied and the subject is held constant. Because of this difference in approach, two types of analyses of neo-Piagetian test data were conducted. In the first, psychometric analyses of the tests and items were obtained for five different age groups separately, as well as for the sample as a whole. The second step consisted of an attempt to test the extent to which the scales were developmentally distributed.

2.1 Psychometric analysis of neo-Piagetian measures. A series of psychometric indices was computed for each of the neo-Piagetian tests. These are: two indices of reliability (the Kuder-Richardson 20 and Cronbach's alpha), Scott's (1960) homogeneity ratio (H.R.), and part/whole correlations.

14

2.1.1 CCS. The CCS was described as consisting of four sub-scales which are directed at different conservation tasks (number, length, substance, weight), and a fifth designed to reflect a subject's level of egocentricity. Table 3 summarizes the psychometric data for these scales. Both KR-20 and Cronbach's alpha were calculated since both of these are based on slightly different assumptions.

TABLE 3. Cartoon Conservation Scales, all sites (N=1189).

Total sample by scale Indices	Number	Length	Substance	Space	Weight		
1. Mean	5.200	5.020	4.580	2.860	2.020		
2. S.D.	1.530	1.600	2.050	2.080	2.170		
3. KR-20	.850	.826	.892	.802	.865		
4. Cronbach's α	.849	.825	.890	.801	.864		
5. H.R.	.487	.447	.575	.402	.516		
6. Part/whole	.781	.754	.835	.614	.557		
Total test by age Indices	Age (expressed in years and months)						
	--7.6	7.7-8.6	8.7-9.6	9.7-10.6	10.7-11.6	11.7+	Total
1. Mean	13.500	16.990	18.480	21.780	22.680	23.820	19.670
2. S.D.	6.610	6.260	6.950	4.370	4.830	4.310	6.600
3. KR-20	.889	.891	.879	.818	.854	.834	.908
4. α	.889	.891	.904	.817	.853	.834	.908
5. H.R.	.212	.217	.242	.145	.177	.166	.253
	N=217	N=155	N=182	N=191	N=168	N=267	N=1180

As may be seen, for each scale individually as well as the five scales together, the reliability values are virtually identical. Over and beyond the issue of reliability, there is a question as to the extent of the internal consistency of the items within each of the five sub-scales. It is well known that reliabilities are influenced by the number of items comprising the test or subscale (Scott 1960). Therefore, an estimate of the internal homogeneity of each scale has been obtained across all of the subscales as well as for the total test. According to Scott (1960), the homogeneity ratio is a conservative index of the average correlation between test items. In practice, ratios between .150 and .600 are acceptable (personal communication with William A. Scott, University of Colorado, 1967). The smaller the value of the ratio, the more complex and heterogeneous is the concept that is being measured by the scale. Values below .150 suggest that each item is a measure of a different concept. Clearly, the results shown on Table 3 indicate that each of the subscales as well as the test total are measuring a unitary concept. As may be seen, the lowest homogeneity ratio shown is .402, which occurs in the egocentricity or space subscale. In fact, rather than appearing on the low side, the homogeneity ratios approach the higher level (.600), indicating that, as opposed to measuring a multifaceted concept, each scale is measuring the concept it claims to be measuring with a high degree of redundancy. In other words, an item or two might be dropped from each of the subscales while retaining the high reliability.

Last, each subscale was correlated with the test total as indicated by the part/whole correlations. The lowest was for the weight concept, which is understandable since it was the most difficult subscale for the entire sample and would have had a restricted variance. These same indices of reliability, homogeneity, etc. were calculated for each of six different age levels independently, as indicated in the second part of Table 3. These calculations, however, were based on the total test. As was the case with the individual subscales, the reliability indices are quite high and there is virtually no difference between the KR-20's and the Cronbach alpha's. On the other hand, however, the homogeneities were slightly lower. These differences between ages are entirely understandable in terms of the changing level of difficulty for each age group; as age increases, the difficulty of the test should decrease. In other words, quality of performance is directly related to age. In summary, there can be little doubt that the CCS holds up as a psychometrically sound instrument across the five different subscales as well as for the test total. This is true for the entire sample as well as for each of the five different age groups.

A second form of analysis of the CCS was conducted by means of a factor analysis. It was a principal components analysis with varimax rotations. The results of this analysis are provided in Table 4.

The factor analysis was done to determine the extent to which the a priori analysis of the scale items matched the empirical analysis. Table 4 shows five factors were extracted. The criterion for factor extraction was an eigenvalue in excess of 1.0. As may be seen, the first factor accounted for 31% of the total variance. The second factor accounted for 11%; the third for 8%; the fourth for 4%; and the fifth for 3%. Altogether, 58.96% of the variance was accounted for. Table 4 shows the factor loading for each item on each factor. Items were boxed on the basis of the highest factor loading for each item. Factor 1 is shown to consist of nine items. The first three items are from the number scale whereas the remaining six constituted the total number of conservation of substance items. Factor 1 can thus be considered as basically a conservation of substance scale. This empirical result matches the hypothesized factor structure with the exception of the three conservation of number items. Factor 2 is made up of virtually all of the conservation of weight items. The factor loadings are all in excess of .66. Turning to Factor 3, it is seen to be comprised entirely of the egocentricity items. Thus, the third factor may be called egocentricity in exactly the same way as the theoretical analysis hypothesized. The fourth factor is also consistent with hypothesized structure. It consists of the six conservation of length items and substantiates the relationship between the theory and empirical results.

TABLE 4. Factor analysis, Conservation Scales, five factors rotated (principal component analysis with varimax rotation).

Variable contents	Factor 1	Factor 2	Factor 3	Factor 4	Factor 5	Communalities H^2
Eigenvalues	9.394	3.387	2.558	1.265	1.085	Total %
% of variance	31.31	11.29	8.53	4.21	3.62	58.96
1) Number-1	.660	.084	.082	-.041	-.181	.483
6) Number-2	.670	.064	.108	-.081	-.318	.572
12) Number-3	.548	.021	.146	-.143	-.475	.568
18) Number-4	.360	.076	.057	-.109	-.695	.634
21) Number-5	.396	.039	.110	-.190	-.717	.721
29) Number-6	.237	.026	.080	-.164	-.768	.680
2) Length-1	.456	.066	.040	-.514	.013	.478
5) Length-2	.212	.077	.056	-.754	-.105	.634
11) Length-3	.208	.054	.078	-.662	-.356	.617
16) Length-4	.419	.071	.039	-.578	-.312	.613
26) Length-5	.374	.073	.031	-.475	-.505*	.626
28) Length-6	.349	.053	.044	-.446	-.438	.680
3) Substance-1	.744	.096	.176	-.189	-.019	.629
7) Substance-2	.709	.116	.122	-.239	-.116	.602
10) Substance-3	.723	.091	.138	-.152	-.247	.634
15) Substance-4	.687	.082	.158	-.178	-.289	.619
17) Substance-5	.654	.093	.149	-.198	-.234	.553
23) Substance-6	.708	.043	.130	-.235	-.249	.638
4) Space-1	.181	.045	.395	.149	-.066	.217
8) Space-2	.061	.057	.630	.084	-.062	.414
14) Space-3	.076	.099	.667	-.063	-.100	.475
22) Space-4	.110	.070	.817	-.146	-.002	.705
25) Space-5	.172	.041	.809	-.129	-.016	.703
27) Space-6	.111	.062	.790	-.144	-.036	.662
9) Weight-1	.205	.669	.029	-.000	.014	.491
13) Weight-2	.203	.664	.154	.029	-.109	.518
19) Weight-3	.023	.814	.058	-.081	-.016	.672
20) Weight-4	-.024	.797	.038	-.123	-.063	.657
24) Weight-5	.004	.846	.024	-.037	-.024	.719
30) Weight-6	.075	.786	.102	-.035	-.010	.637

The fifth factor extracted consists of the remaining three conservation of number items, with the exception of item 26, which was a conservation of length item (it is noted by an asterisk). In summary, it can be said that there was substantial agreement between the a priori and empirical levels of analysis. Out of 30 items, 26 fell into the hypothesized subscale or factor. With the exception of the first three conservation of number items and the fifth conservation of length item, all other items fell into their hypothesized grouping.

2.1.2 WLT. The WLT is made up of three basic scales or subscales. The items are composed of vertical-horizontal, tilted, and three-dimensional bottles. Table 5 shows means, standard deviations, Cronbach alpha's, homogeneity ratios, and part/whole correlations for each subscale of the WLT as well as across six different age levels. As may be seen, the reliability for each subscale is at least at .828.

The part/whole correlation was lowest for the tilted bottles at .781. The homogeneities are all quite high with respect to age groups. It can be seen that both reliabilities and homogeneities hold up for each age group separately as well as for the total sample. Total reliability for the test is .884 while the homogeneity is .333, both well within acceptable limits.

TABLE 5. Water Level Task, all sites (N=1189).

Indices	Vertical/horizontal	Tilted	3-dimensional				
1. Mean	6.640	3.260	2.290				
2. S.D.	2.380	2.120	1.530				
3. Cronbach's α	.828	.916	.801				
4. H.R.	.573	.577	.338				
5. Part/whole	.825	.781	.791				
Indices	Age (given in years and months)						
	--7.6	7.7-8.6	8.7-9.6	9.7-10.6	10.7-11.6	11.7+	Total
1. Mean	8.000	9.640	11.610	12.840	14.170	15.760	12.190
2. S.D.	4.400	4.150	4.000	3.870	4.050	3.340	4.820
3. α	.826	.809	.833	.852	.871	.839	.884
4. H.R.	.328	.260	.246	.248	.275	.217	.333

A second analysis was conducted in which an attempt was made to test the empirical versus the theoretical relationships among items. A factor analysis conducted in the same manner as that conducted on the CCS was performed. The results of these analyses are summarized in Table 6. Three factors were extracted using the same criterion of an eigenvalue in excess of 1. The first factor accounted for 36.8% of the total variance. Items are boxed according to their highest loading on any given factor.

Factor 1 consists of the eight tilted bottles, a perfect replication of the conceptual scale. Factor 2 consists of the four vertical-horizontal along with two of the three-dimensional bottles. The two three-dimensional bottles in the factor were in horizontal orientation indicating that the three-dimensional aspect was overlooked and the items were responded to in the same way as the two-dimensional vertical-horizontal bottles. Factor 3 is made up of six of the eight three-dimensional bottles. These three factors accounted for 58.71% of the total variance. The analysis, which constitutes a form of construct validation, also supports the notion that the empirically generated scales (i.e. factors) match the theoretical scales. Of the twenty original items, only two failed to load most heavily on their theoretically appropriate scale.

TABLE 6.   Factor analysis, Water Level Task, three factors rotated (principal component with varimax rotation).

Variable	Factor 1	Factor 2	Factor 3	H²
Eigenvalues	7.363	2.450	1.929	Total % of variance
% of Variance	36.81	12.26	9.10	58.71
1. V/H #1, page 2	.013	-.738	.096	.554
2. V/H #2, page 5	.038	-.767	.093	.598
3. V/H #3, page 8	.235	-.810	.138	.730
4. V/H #4, page 21	.221	-.797	.133	.702
5. Tilted #1, page 3	.704	-.210	.130	.557
6. Tilted #2, page 6	.719	-.144	.072	.543
7. Tilted #3, page 9	.761	-.111	.187	.626
8. Tilted #4, page 11	.827	-.164	.117	.725
9. Tilted #5, page 12	.780	-.173	.196	.708
10. Tilted #6, page 14	.790	-.156	.123	.663
11. Tilted #7, page 16	.760	-.075	.151	.606
12. Tilted #8, page 18	.763	-.129	.147	.620
13. 3-D #1, page 4	.181	-.141	.627	.448
14. 3-D #2, page 7	.020	-.106	.687	.484
15. 3-D #3, page 10	.340	-.670*	.232	.617
16. 3-D #4, page 13	.126	-.097	.672	.476
17. 3-D #5, page 15	.125	-.062	.669	.467
18. 3-D #6, page 17	.158	-.140	.667	.490
19. 3-D #7, page 19	.175	-.175	.659	.496
20. 3-D #8, page 20	.334	-.681*	.237	.631

*Horizontal 3-D bottle

2.1.3 FIT and ST. A series of similar analyses were conducted with the FIT and ST. An examination of the FIT as shown in Table 7 reveals that the reliabilities and homogeneities are high for each age group as well as for the total sample. On the other hand, it may be seen that the homogeneity of the ST is quite low (.108). This ST result generates some question as to the reliability of the ST in its present format. The same question arises through an examination of the ST reliabilities.

At this point it should be noted that the version of the ST employed differs slightly from the version previously used by De Avila (1972). De Avila (1972) used small geometrical shapes with nine different colors as the basic repertoire from which stimulus elements were sampled. The present version involved a series of slides, each having a colored drawing of a different object (car, hat, burro, etc.). These objects may have different saliency values than the geometric shapes. If this were true, it would perhaps account for the lower homogeneity and the overall lower reliability.

Another problem encountered by some test administrators, which may have a bearing on the basically poor psychometric status of the ST, was that the slide projector had to be manually operated. In

TABLE 7. Figural Intersection Task and Serial Task, all sites (N=1180).

Indices	Age (expressed in years and months)						Total
	--7.6	7.7-8.6	8.7-9.6	9.7-10.6	10.7-11.6	11.7+	
	Figural Intersection Task						
1. Mean	12.900	16.110	17.190	19.800	21.620	23.510	18.750
2. S.D.	7.230	6.920	6.970	7.050	6.260	6.140	7.720
3. Cronbach	.911	.897	.902	.912	.892	.908	.926
4. H.R.	.259	.227	.238	.263	.225	.263	.300
	Serial Task						
1. Mean	2.950	3.300	3.800	4.490	5.170	5.230	4.210
2. S.D.	2.320	1.990	1.970	2.000	2.260	2.200	2.320
3. α	.691	.576	.545	.520	.590	.585	.645
4. H.R.	.141	.099	.088	.069	.084	.081	.108
	N=217	N=155	N=182	N=190	N=169	N=267	N=1180

presenting a series of five or six slides, the experimenter had to count the individual slides as they were flashed on the screen, remembering to stop at the end of the sequence. For some experimenters, this proved to be somewhat difficult, and there were a number of complaints having to do with the procedure. A later examination of site differences showed that there were some experimenter effects, suggesting that ability to manipulate the machine seemed to have some effect which was ultimately translated into performance.

A factor analytic examination of the ST further confirmed the fact that the ST is not viable in its present form. Five factors were extracted, in total accounting for only 37% of the total variance. The first factor, accounting for 13.41% of the variance, is composed primarily of those stimuli containing three stimulus elements. The remaining factors failed to be composed in any way which was consistent with a priori stimulus construction; a result giving rise to additional question concerning the basic viability of the test.

An overview of the psychometric properties of the four neo-Piagetian tasks indicates the CCS and the WLT to be the most psychometrically sound. While the FIT showed slightly lower homogeneity, it nevertheless showed high reliability across all of the age groups and, in fact, showed the highest total reliability of the four tests. The ST in its present form showed itself to be less sound than the other three tasks, with middle range reliability and very low homogeneity.

2.2 Developmental properties of neo-Piagetian measures. The developmental properties of the four neo-Piagetian tests were examined by conducting two basic analyses. First, intercorrelations between the

TABLE 8. Factor analysis, Serial Task (types 3–7 slides), five factors rotated (principal component with varimax rotation).

Variable	Type	Sequence	Factor 1	Factor 2	Factor 3	Factor 4	Factor 5	H²
Eigenvalue			2.68	1.35	1.23	1.15	1.11	Total % of variance
% of variance			13.41	6.76	6.17	5.74	5.53	37.61
3)	3–slides	5	.443	.129	.098	.007	.089	.230
9)	3–slides	12	.602	-.016	-.025	-.039	-.013	.365
18)	3–slides	24	.625	-.063	-.032	-.057	-.097	.409
20)	3–slides	27	.553	.093	-.033	.020	.048	.318
2)	4–slides	4	.254	-.028	-.232	-.090	.280	.205
7)	4–slides	10	.502	.108	-.178	-.030	.173	.326
10)	4–slides	13	.266	-.018	-.433	.096	.077	.274
16)	4–slides	21	.513	.037	-.295	-.040	.047	.355
1)	5–slides	2	.118	.186	-.453	.129	.055	.273
4)	5–slides	6	.116	.551	-.084	.125	.353	.530
11)	5–slides	14	.032	.149	-.487	-.210	.092	.313
13)	5–slides	17	.194	.056	-.326	-.244	.503	.460
5)	6–slides	7	-.069	-.066	-.430	-.558	-.159	.530
6)	6–slides	9	-.049	-.057	-.601	.049	-.035	.370
12)	6–slides	16	.047	.579	-.151	-.072	-.175	.396
14)	6–slides	19	.055	.623	.045	-.063	.116	.411
8)	7–slides	11	.042	.402	-.087	-.082	-.389	.329
15)	7–slides	20	.125	-.052	.076	-.708	.189	.561
17)	7–slides	22	.006	.063	.006	-.007	.700	.495
19)	7–slides	25	.019	.318	.154	-.557	-.021	.437

four tests and chronological age were obtained. Second, performance on each of the four tests was plotted as a function of age. To carry out these analyses, the total sample was divided into six age groups in the same way as was done for the psychometric analyses described above. Since the four tests were scored slightly differently, it was necessary to transform scores into a standard score. This was done by dichotomizing each item (right = 1 and wrong = 0) and treating scores in terms of the probability of a correct response.

An examination was made of the interrelationship of the four neo-Piagetian tests along with chronological age. Table 9 shows the intercorrelation of these five variables. All correlations are significant beyond the .001 level. A second set of correlations was done across all of the individual test subscales. These may be found in Table 10.

TABLE 9. Correlations (N=1180).

	CA	CCS	WLT	FIT
CCS	.547			
WLT	.560	.535		
FIT	.474	.470	.544	
ST	.389	.392	.340	.334

TABLE 10. Total sample: Correlations among neo-Piagetian measures.

	Chronological age	CCS number	CCS length	CCS substance	CCS space	CCS weight	CCS total	WLT V/H	WLT tilt	WLT 3-D	WLT total	ST total
CCS number	.344											
CCS length	.299	.687										
CCS substance	.488	.737	.687									
CCS space	.465	.290	.235	.354								
CCS weight	.225	.188	.204	.236	.196							
CCS total	.564	.745	.708	.821	.642	.593						
WLT V/H	.406	.341	.289	.351	.335	.174	.440					
WLT tilt	.434	.235	.244	.281	.398	.219	.519	.367				
WLT 3-D	.457	.250	.262	.332	.396	.201	.516	.525	.465			
WLT total	.560	.358	.340	.407	.468	.202	.541	.822	.774	.789		
FIT total	.474	.343	.295	.415	.390	.249	.430	.434	.441	.431	.544	
ST total	.389	.329	.280	.355	.287	.202	.401	.296	.239	.264	.340	.344

p < .05, r=.195; p < .01, r=.254; p < .001, r=.321

Again, all of the correlations are statistically significant, thus demonstrating a high degree of interrelation between rather diverse procedural methods.

A number of analyses were conducted across the five different age groups in order to determine the extent to which the items, subscales, and tests were developmentally distributed. The developmental hypothesis suggests that there would be a linear relationship between age and probability of correct response.

Figure 1 shows the probability of a correct response for each of the different subscales of the CCS across six different age groups.

FIGURE 1. Conservation Scales, probability of correct response (N=1254)

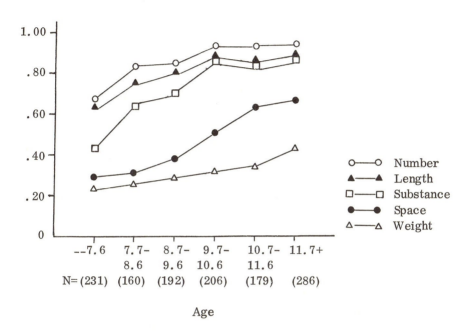

It should be noted that the rank order of difficulty for each of the item types or subscale types is consistent with Piaget's functional analysis of conservation. Conservation of number and length were of equal difficulty and both were somewhat easier than substance. The most difficult were the egocentricity or the space items and conservation of weight. This is consistent with Piaget's analysis (1952) and suggests a consistency between Piaget's clinical method and the cartoon format employed by the CCS.

Figure 2 shows the plot for Pascual-Leone's WLT. The same basic results were obtained as for the CCS. First, each of the subscales is developmentally distributed, that is, there is a basically linear relationship between age and performance. Second, the rank order of item difficulty or subscale difficulty is consistent with Pascual-Leone's analysis of task difficulty.

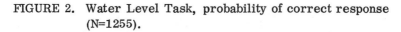

FIGURE 2.   Water Level Task, probability of correct response
(N=1255).

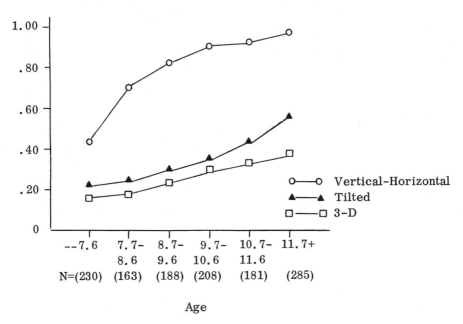

Age

    Analyses of individual subscales were not conducted on either the
FIT or ST because these tests do not contain subscales in the same
sense as the CCS and WLT.
    An attempt was made to examine the relationship between age and
total test performance on each of the four neo-Piagetian tests. It may
be seen in Figure 3 that three of the four tests (CCS, WLT, and FIT)
show an almost linear relation between age and performance. Furthermore, the curves for CCS, WLT, and FIT across the six age groups
are almost identical. The relation of age and performance on the ST,
on the other hand, was less than expected. The slope of the developmental curve was flatter for ST than for the other three tests.
    In summary, the above analyses show that with minor exceptions
three of the four neo-Piagetian tests are developmentally sound. The
analysis of relation between age and performance shows, as expected,
that there is a direct relation between the two. Moreover, the rank
order of item or task difficulty is consistent with Piagetian developmental theory.

FIGURE 3. Neo-Piagetian tests, total scores, probability of correct response (N=1180).

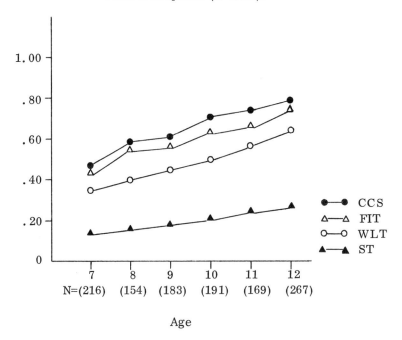

CHAPTER 3

FOUR SITE ANALYSES

In the following pages results of the analysis of data collected at
each site can be found, presented site by site. The rationale for the
organization of the results in such a manner rests on two basic facts:
first, each of the four sites is extremely different from the others and
warrants an individual examination of data; and second, the standardized capacity and achievement tests employed vary from site to site,
making it impossible to examine all sites together with respect to
these tests. When aspects of the data lend themselves to across-
site comparisons, these comparisons were, in fact, performed and
may be found in the next chapter.

The data analysis procedure for each site was similar and is presented in generally the same format. First, the sampling procedure,
the sample, and the method of instrument administration are discussed. Second, a description of sample performance (means and
standard deviations) is presented for both developmental and standardized measures, grade by grade. Although the entire sample results
on the developmental measures have already been discussed on an
age-group basis, the data for the individual sites are examined grade-
by-grade because the standardized capacity and achievement measures
were administered according to grade. Third, correlations of developmental with standardized measures (also including chronological age
and sex) are presented if they were performed on groups large enough
to render such correlations meaningful. Finally, the results at each
site were examined for sex differences. The technique used was
analysis of variance. At one of the four sites there was a sufficient
number of Anglo-American children tested to allow for the examination
of ethnic group differences via an analysis of variance.

26

3.1 New Mexico

3.1.1 Sample and procedure. The New Mexico sample consisted
of children attending one elementary school in an area which is predominantly Mexican-American (approximately 75% Spanish-surnamed).
Each grade group was composed of two entire classrooms; there was
no subsampling within the classrooms. There were two test administrators, one male and one female. All tests, both developmental
neo-Piagetian and standardized, were administered in English.

The developmental neo-Piagetian measures were administered as
previously described. The children in grades one and two received
the measures in groups of two to five children. The standardized
achievement and intelligence tests were administered according to
publisher's directions. The standardized tests including levels and
forms administered at this site may be found in Table 11.

TABLE 11. Standardized tests administered in New Mexico.

Grade 1	Stanford Early School Achievement Test (SESAT), Level II Otis-Lennon Mental Ability Test, Primary II
Grade 2	Comprehensive Test of Basic Skills (CTBS), Level I Otis-Lennon Mental Ability Test, Elementary I
Grade 3	CTBS, Level I Otis-Lennon, Elementary I
Grade 4	CTBS, Level II, form R Otis-Lennon, Elementary II
Grade 5	CTBS, Level II, form Q Otis-Lennon, Elementary II
Grade 6	CTBS, Level II, form Q Otis-Lennon, Elementary II

3.1.2 Results

3.1.2.1 Group performance. The performance of the New Mexico
sample will be discussed grade by grade rather than age group by age
group because the standardized tests vary from grade to grade and not
from age group to age group. Unfortunately, having the data in this
form obscures some age group differences, especially considering
that in each grade there are children who are either overage for that

grade or children who are underage. However, since these matters were necessarily under the control of the site personnel, there was nothing that could be done about this occurrence. Fortunately, New Mexico was one of the sites where the percentage of children overage or underage for their grade was relatively low.

Inspection of Tables 12 and 13 reveals several things. First, it can be seen that the performance of the children on the capacity measures is roughly average. The performance on the achievement measures

TABLE 12. New Mexico grades 1, 2, and 3: Performance on developmental, capacity, and achievement measures.

	Grade 1 n=52		Grade 2 n=55		Grade 3 n=63	
	Mean	SD	Mean	SD	Mean	SD
Chronological age (in years and months)	6-6	-6	7-6	-7	8-8	-9
Developmental measure (number in parentheses represents total items in each scale)						
CCS/number (6)	5.25	1.44	5.53	1.03	5.06	1.72
CCS/length (6)	4.92	1.61	4.82	1.69	4.94	1.55
CCS/substance (6)	4.62	2.04	4.14	2.42	4.25	2.07
CCS/space (6)	3.06	2.09	1.45	1.66	3.19	1.80
CCS/weight (6)	1.83	2.09	1.44	1.93	1.57	1.94
WLT/total score (20)	6.33	3.52	7.34	3.90	11.22	4.13
FIT/total score (30)	12.41	5.22	17.05	7.56	19.57	11.73
ST/total score (20)	8.94	2.48	10.71	2.33	11.62	2.27
Capacity measure						
SESAT (national percentile)	24.40	--	--	--	--	--
CTBS total (grade equivalent)	--	--	2.08	.89	2.77	1.33

TABLE 13. New Mexico grades 4, 5, and 6: Performance on developmental, capacity, and achievement measures.

	Grade 4 n=67		Grade 5 n=61		Grade 6 n=69	
	Mean	SD	Mean	SD	Mean	SD
Chronological age (in years and months)	9-7	-7	10-8	-7	11-8	-8
Developmental measure (numbers in parentheses represent total items in each scale)						
CCS/number (6)	5.45	.89	5.62	.82	5.84	.53
CCS/length (6)	5.00	1.41	5.07	1.52	5.59	.79
CCS/substance (6)	5.13	1.47	5.02	1.64	5.81	.46
CCS/space (6)	3.22	1.88	4.33	1.85	4.52	1.44
CCS/weight (6)	1.55	1.89	2.03	2.11	2.93	2.36
WLT/weight (20)	11.86	1.21	14.17	4.07	15.98	3.24
FIT/total (20)	23.09	7.37	25.00	6.89	27.18	6.88
ST/total (30)	12.22	2.85	13.56	2.26	13.35	2.37
Capacity measure						
Otis-Lennon mental age	8.90	1.80	10.40	1.76	11.47	1.85
Otis-Lennon DIQ	95.61	14.40	99.34	13.44	101.67	14.35
Achievement measure						
CTBS total (grade equivalent)	3.24	1.80	4.35	1.48	5.17	2.91

tends to be low with respect to national norms, with the first grade falling in the 24th percentile on the SESAT, grades three, four, five, and six being approximately one grade equivalent behind in their performance on the CTBS. With respect to the neo-Piagetian measures, it can be seen that the test scores do reflect developmental variation, that the scores tend to improve as age increases. Furthermore, the variance tends to decrease as age increases. For example, the score on CCS/substance ranges from a mean of 4.62 and a standard deviation of 2.04 for the grade one children to a mean of 5.81 with a standard deviation of 0.46 for the grade six children. The few aberrations which occur are considered attributable to the fact that these are grade-group performance means as opposed to age-group performance means.

3.1.2.2 Age, sex, and ethnic group differences. After examining the site's performance, differences within the sample were examined. These differences fall into three categories: age, sex, and ethnic group. An examination of ethnic group differences was possible at this site because approximately one-quarter of the sample was Anglo-American.

3.1.2.2.1 Neo-Piagetian measures. A series of ANOVAs, age-by-sex-by-ethnicity, were performed on all the subscales of the developmental neo-Piagetian measures. A summary of the significant F ratios obtained by these ANOVAs may be found in Table 14. An examination of the main effects on this table yields the finding that in addition to strong age-group differences--as expected--several of the developmental measures exhibit sex differences in performance. It also may be seen that there are no ethnic group differences in performance on the developmental neo-Piagetian measures.

Examining the interactions yields the following. First, there are no age by sex interactions and no age by sex by ethnicity interactions,

TABLE 14. New Mexico developmental three-way analysis of variance of neo-Piagetian measures by age, sex, ethnicity (N=402): Significant F ratios.

	CCS number	CCS length	CCS substance	CCS space	CCS weight	CCS total	WLT V/H	WLT tilted	WLT 3-D	WLT total	FIT total	ST total
A (age)	.001	.001	.001	.001	.001	.001	.001	.001	.001	.001	.001	.001
B (sex)	NS	NS	NS	.001	NS	.05	NS	.05	NS	.05	.025	NS
C (ethnicity)	NS	NS	NS	NS	NS	NS	NS	NS	NS	NS	NS	NS
AB (age/sex)	NS	NS	NS	NS	NS	NS	NS	NS	NS	NS	NS	NS
AC (age/eth.)	NS	.005	.025	NS	NS	NS	NS	NS	NS	NS	NS	.005
BC (sex/eth.)	NS	NS	NS	.05	NS	NS	NS	NS	NS	NS	NS	NS
ABC	NS	NS	NS	NS	NS	NS	NS	NS	NS	NS	NS	NS

but there is a single sex by ethnicity interaction. While the significant main effects attributed to sex and the effect of interactions of ethnicity with other variables in performance are of interest, the age differences are of no real theoretical interest as these were built into the scales.

The specific ANOVA tables for all those ANOVAs producing significant F's (other than age) can be found in Tables 15-22. The first of these is CCS/length (Table 15).

TABLE 15. New Mexico, all subjects, CCS/length: Analysis of variance by age, sex, ethnicity.

	SS	df	MS	F
Age (A)	5.46	5	1.09	5.78**
Sex (B)	.16	1	.16	.86
Ethnicity (C)	.10	1	.10	.54
A x B	.36	5	.07	.38
A x C	3.20	5	.64	3.39*
B x C	.00	1	.00	.00
A x B x C	.91	5	.18	.97
Within	71.33	378	.19	

*p < .05
**p < .001

As may be seen, there is a main effect of age significant at .001 level. In addition, there is a significant interaction of age with ethnic group. Although no post hoc comparisons were performed, the cell means indicate that the Anglo-American children in the youngest and the three oldest age groups performed at higher cognitive levels than their Mexican-American counterparts, while in the two remaining intermediate age groups the Mexican-American children performed at higher cognitive levels than the Anglo-American children.

Table 16 provides the ANOVA for CCS/substance. As before, in addition to a significant main effect of age, there is an interaction of age with ethnic group. Interestingly enough, this interaction is exactly the same as on the previous subscale: in the youngest and the three oldest age groups the Anglo-American children perform better than the Mexican-American, and in the two intermediate age groups the Mexican-American children are the superior performers.

A summary of the CCS/space ANOVA may be found in Table 17. In this case there are two significant main effects--age and sex--and a statistically significant interaction between sex and ethnicity. The sex difference indicates that males perform better than females. The sex-ethnicity interaction is such that the Anglo-American males are

TABLE 16. New Mexico, all subjects, CCS/substance: Analysis of variance by age, sex, ethnicity.

	SS	df	MS	F
Age (A)	24.55	5	4.91	17.54**
Sex (B)	.07	1	.07	.27
Ethnicity (C)	.06	1	.06	.22
A x B	1.01	5	.20	.72
A x C	3.94	5	.79	2.82*
B x C	.09	1	.09	.31
A x B x C	1.48	5	.30	1.06
Within	105.78	378	.28	

*p < .025
**p < .001

TABLE 17. New Mexico, all subjects, CCS/space: Analysis of variance by age, sex, ethnicity.

	SS	df	MS	F
Age (A)	33.36	5	6.67	27.67**
Sex (B)	4.74	1	4.74	19.67**
Ethnicity (C)	.32	1	.32	1.35
A x B	1.65	5	.33	1.37
A x C	.28	5	.06	.23
B x C	1.06	1	1.06	4.38*
A x B x C	1.20	5	.24	.99
Within	91.14	378	.24	

*p < .05
**p < .001

the most cognitively advanced performers on this scale, followed by the Mexican-American males, followed by the Mexican-American females, followed by the Anglo-American females.

With respect to the total score on the CCS, there again is a significant main effect of age and a significant main effect of sex. These two may be seen in Table 18. Cell totals indicate that the males perform at a more advanced cognitive level than do the females.

The same sex difference is to be found in performance on the WLT tilted bottle scale; that is, the males' performance was at a higher cognitive level than the females'. The summary of this ANOVA may be found in Table 19.

TABLE 18. New Mexico, all subjects, CCS total score: Analysis of variance by age, sex, ethnicity.

	SS	df	MS	F
Age (A)	327.13	5	65.43	27.18**
Sex (B)	11.23	1	11.23	4.66*
Ethnicity (C)	.03	1	.03	.01
A x B	6.43	5	1.29	.53
A x C	22.31	5	4.46	1.85
B x C	5.27	1	5.27	2.19
A x B x C	19.82	5	3.96	1.65
Within	909.84	378	2.41	

*p < .05
**p < .001

TABLE 19. New Mexico, all subjects, WLT/tilted bottles: Analysis of variance by age, sex, ethnicity.

	SS	df	MS	F
Age (A)	27.90	5	5.58	19.23**
Sex (B)	1.14	1	1.14	3.92*
Ethnicity (C)	.17	1	.17	.57
A x B	.97	5	.19	.67
A x C	1.98	5	.40	1.37
B x C	.28	1	.28	.97
A x B x C	.47	5	.09	.32
Within	109.70	378	.29	

*p < .05
**p < .001

TABLE 20. New Mexico, all subjects, WLT total score: Analysis of variance by age, sex, ethnicity.

	SS	df	MS	F
Age (A)	244.81	5	48.96	37.35**
Sex (B)	5.21	1	5.21	3.98*
Ethnicity (C)	1.72	1	1.72	1.31
A x B	2.01	5	.40	.31
A x C	5.50	5	1.10	.84
B x C	.02	1	.02	.02
A x B x C	6.76	5	1.35	1.03
Within	495.54			

*p < .05
**p < .001

In Table 20, one again sees the same sex differences on the total score of the WLT. This sex difference is repeated on the total score of the FIT.

Table 22 contains the summary of the ANOVA on the total score of the ST. Examining this table, it can be seen that there is a significant interaction between age and ethnicity. The performance of the two ethnic groups indicates no particular pattern. In some of the age groups the Anglo-American children perform better than the Mexican-American children; in other age groups the effect is reversed; and in two of the six age groups the performance is essentially the same for both ethnic groups.

TABLE 21. New Mexico, all subjects, FIT total score: Analysis of variance by age, sex, ethnicity.

	SS	df	MS	F
Age (A)	581.18	5	116.24	23.12**
Sex (B)	29.11	1	29.11	5.79*
Ethnicity (C)	.00	1	.00	.00
A x B	19.43	5	3.89	.77
A x C	21.75	5	4.35	.87
B x C	.01	1	.01	.00
A x B x C	28.81	5	5.76	1.15
Within	1900.75	378	5.03	

*p < .025
**p < .001

TABLE 22. New Mexico, all subjects, ST total score: Analysis of variance by age, sex, ethnicity.

	SS	df	MS	F
Age (A)	61.33	5	12.27	25.07**
Sex (B)	.04	1	.04	.09
Ethnicity (C)	1.10	1	1.10	2.25
A x B	1.14	5	.23	.47
A x C	8.80	5	1.76	3.60*
B x C	.00	1	.00	.00
A x B x C	3.04	5	.61	1.24
Within	184.98	378	.49	

*p < .005
**p < .001

In summarizing these differences on the developmental measures it may be said that in addition to the built-in age group differences, there tend to be some sex differences. When there are sex differences they indicate more advanced cognitive levels of males as compared to females. Furthermore, there occasionally are interactions of either age or sex with ethnicity.

3.1.2.2.2 Capacity and achievement measures. ANOVAs were also computed on the standardized capacity and achievement measures. They were computed in the following way: grade one was analyzed by itself, as it was the only one to which the SESAT was administered. As only one grade was involved, a sex by ethnic group ANOVA was performed. As it was felt that age would not vary enough within one grade, age was not included as a variable. Table 23 is a summary of results of the two-way ANOVAs performed on the grade one data.

TABLE 23. New Mexico grade 1, Otis-Lennon primary II level and SESAT level II: Analysis of variance by sex, ethnicity (N=53).

Otis-Lennon, primary II level, form J					
	M. A.		IQ		
Sex (A)	NS		NS		
Ethnic group (B)	.025		.05		
AB	NS		NS		
Stanford Early School Achievement Test, Level II					
				Reading	
	Environment	Math	Letters	Aural	Word	Sentence
Sex (A)	NS	NS	NS	NS	NS	NS
Ethnic group (B)	NS	NS	NS	.025	NS	NS
AB	NS	NS	NS	NS	NS	NS

First, it may be seen that on the capacity measure, the Otis-Lennon Mental Abilities Test, there was a significant main effect of ethnicity on the mental age and also on the deviation IQ score (DIQ). Summary of the Otis-Lennon analyses may be found in Table 24. The direction of the ethnic group difference is in favor of the Anglo-American children. This finding is interesting in light of the fact that there were no ethnic group main effects on the developmental neo-Piagetian measures. Second, the Stanford Early School Achievement Test (SESAT) aural comprehension subtest has an ethnic group difference in favor of the Anglo-American children. The specifics of this ANOVA may be found in Table 25.

TABLE 24. New Mexico grade 1, Otis-Lennon mental age, DIQ.

	Mental age				DIQ			
	SS	df	MS	F	SS	df	MS	F
Sex (A)	.12	1	.12	1.72	10.33	1	10.33	.75
Ethnicity (B)	.47	1	.47	6.45**	65.58	1	65.58	4.77*
A x B	.01	1	.01	.08	1.38	1	1.38	.10
Within	3.46	48	.07		659.93	48	13.75	

*p < .05
**p < .025

TABLE 25. New Mexico grade 1, SESAT aural comprehension: Analysis of variance by sex, ethnicity.

	SS	df	MS	F
Sex (A)	.64	1	.64	.63
Ethnicity (B)	6.50	1	6.50	6.37*
A x B	.22	1	.22	.22
Within	48.98	48	1.02	

*p < .025

The next series of ANOVAs was conducted on grades two and three together because they received the same levels and forms of the Otis-Lennon Mental Abilities Test and the CTBS. A summary of the significant F ratios may be found in Table 26. Examination of the upper part of Table 26 shows that there is an ethnic group difference on Part 3 of the Otis-Lennon. Cell means indicate that the Anglo-American children perform better than do the Mexican-American children. The ANOVA itself may be found in Table 27. The lower part of Table 26 is devoted to the CTBS. While there are no ethnic group differences on the CTBS, there are some sex differences primarily in the first part of the test which concerns verbs and language skills. There is also one interaction of sex and ethnic group. The specifics of these ANOVAs may be found in Tables 27-32.

The first CTBS scale exhibiting a sex difference is that of vocabulary: females scored significantly higher than males. Furthermore, there is an interaction of sex and ethnic group. The nature of the sex-ethnicity interaction is such that Mexican-American males scored higher than Anglo-American males and Anglo-American females scored higher than Mexican-American females. The order of their performance is as follows: the Anglo-American females

TABLE 26. New Mexico grades 2 and 3, standardized tests: Analysis of variance by age, sex, ethnicity (N=118).

Otis-Lennon Mental Ability Test, Elementary I level, form J

	M. A.	IQ	Part 1	Part 2	Part 3
A (age)	.05	.01	NS	NS	.025
B (sex)	NS	NS	NS	NS	NS
C (ethnic group)	NS	NS	NS	NS	.025
A x B	NS	NS	NS	NS	NS
A x C	NS	NS	NS	NS	NS
B x C	NS	NS	NS	NS	NS
A x B x C	NS	NS	NS	NS	NS

Comprehensive Test of Basic Skills, level I, form Q

	Vocabulary	Comprehension	Mechanics	Expression	Spelling	Arithmetic computation	Arithmetic concepts	Arithmetic application	Total	Study skills
A (age)	.05	NS	.01	.025	.01	.001	.01	NS	NS	.05
B (sex)	.01	.01	.01	.005	.001	NS	NS	NS	NS	NS
C (ethnic group)	NS	NS	NS	NS	NS	NS	NS	NS	NS	NS
A x B	NS	NS	NS	NS	NS	NS	NS	NS	NS	NS
A x C	NS	NS	NS	NS	NS	NS	NS	NS	NS	NS
B x C	.05	NS	NS	NS	NS	NS	NS	NS	NS	NS
A x B x C	NS	NS	NS	NS	NS	NS	NS	NS	NS	NS

TABLE 27. New Mexico grades 2 and 3, Otis-Lennon mental ability test, part III scores: Analysis of variance by age, sex, ethnicity.

	SS	df	MS	F
Age (A)	14.46	1	14.46	6.49*
Sex (B)	.05	1	.05	.02
Ethnicity (C)	13.20	1	13.20	5.93*
A x B	.44	1	.44	.20
A x C	.84	1	.84	.38
B x C	.01	1	.01	.01
A x B x C	1.86	1	1.86	.83
Within	245.06	110	2.23	

*$p < .025$

scored higher than Mexican-American females. The order of their performance is as follows: the Anglo-American females are the best performers, followed by the Mexican-American females, followed by Spanish-surnamed males, followed by Anglo-American males. The ANOVA may be found in Table 28.

The ANOVA on the CTBS Comprehension Scale yields a sex difference indicating females performing superior to males (Table 29). It
is interesting to note there is no age difference on this scale.

TABLE 28. New Mexico grades 2 and 3, CTBS/vocabulary:
Analysis of variance by age, sex, ethnicity.

	SS	df	MS	F
Age (A)	27.70	1	27.70	4.72*
Sex (B)	47.32	1	47.32	8.06**
Ethnicity (C)	2.95	1	2.95	.50
A x B	2.92	1	2.92	.50
A x C	2.66	1	2.66	.45
B x C	23.50	1	23.50	4.00*
A x B x C	6.12	1	6.12	1.04
Within	645.96	110	5.87	

*p < .05
**p < .01

TABLE 29. New Mexico grades 2 and 3, CTBS/comprehension:
Analysis of variance by age, sex, ethnicity.

	SS	df	MS	F
Age (A)	22.18	1	22.18	2.37
Sex (B)	71.89	1	71.89	7.67*
Ethnicity (C)	.05	1	.05	.01
A x B	2.89	1	2.89	.31
A x C	3.87	1	3.87	.41
B x C	9.79	1	9.79	1.04
A x B x C	13.59	1	13.59	1.45
Within	1030.57	110	13.59	

*p < .01

With respect to the next three subtests--language mechanics,
expression, and spelling--one finds the same sex difference as before
(see Tables 30, 31, and 32).

The forms and levels of the standardized tests administered to
grades four, five, and six were the same, which allowed these grades
to be analyzed together. A series of three-way ANOVAs (age, sex,
and ethnic group) were performed on the Otis-Lennon and on the CTBS.
A summary of these ANOVAs may be found in Table 33. As with grades
two and three, there are ethnic group differences on the capacity

TABLE 30. New Mexico grades 2 and 3, CTBS/language
mechanics: Analysis of variance by age, sex,
ethnicity.

	SS	df	MS	F
Age (A)	21.33	1	21.33	7.59*
Sex (B)	22.31	1	22.31	7.94*
Ethnicity (C)	.15	1	.15	.05
A x B	4.94	1	4.94	1.76
A x C	.08	1	.08	.03
B x C	3.11	1	3.11	1.10
A x B x C	3.48	1	3.48	1.24
Within	309.23	110	2.81	

*$p < .01$

TABLE 31. New Mexico grades 2 and 3, CTBS/expression:
analysis of variance by age, sex, ethnicity.

	SS	df	MS	F
Age (A)	24.55	1	24.55	5.46*
Sex (B)	41.31	1	41.31	9.19**
Ethnicity (C)	2.86	1	2.86	.64
A x B	.98	1	.98	.22
A x C	.51	1	.51	.11
B x C	.87	1	.87	.19
A x B x C	4.14	1	4.14	.92
Within	494.65	110	4.50	

*$p < .025$
**$p < .005$

TABLE 32. New Mexico grades 2 and 3, CTBS/spelling:
Analysis of variance by age, sex, ethnicity.

	SS	df	MS	F
Age (A)	31.32	1	31.32	7.25*
Sex (B)	73.66	1	73.66	17.05**
Ethnicity (C)	2.48	1	2.48	.57
A x B	2.65	1	2.65	.61
A x C	.00	1	.00	.00
B x C	3.34	1	3.34	.77
A x B x C	2.05	1	2.05	.47
Within	475.32	110	4.32	

*$p < .01$
**$p < .001$

TABLE 33. New Mexico grades 4, 5, and 6, standardized tests: Analysis of variance by age, sex, ethnicity (N=197).

Otis-Lennon Mental Ability Test, Elementary II level, form J		
	Mental age	DIQ
A (age)	.001	NS
B (sex)	NS	NS
C (ethnic group)	NS	.05
A x B	NS	NS
A x C	.01	NS
B x C	NS	NS
A x B x C	NS	NS

Comprehensive Test of Basic Skills, level II, forms Q & R										
	Vocabulary	Comprehension	Mechanics	Expression	Spelling	Arithmetic computation	Concepts	Application	Total	Study skills
A (age)	.001	.005	.001	.005	.001	.01	.001	.001	.005	.001
B (sex)	NS	NS	NS	NS	NS	NS	NS	NS	NS	NS
C (ethnic group)	NS	NS	NS	NS	NS	NS	.01	.025	.05	.025
A x B	NS	NS	NS	NS	NS	NS	NS	NS	NS	NS
A x C	NS	NS	NS	NS	NS	NS	NS	NS	NS	NS
B x C	NS	.01	NS	.025	NS	NS	NS	NS	.05	.05
A x B x C	NS	NS	NS	NS	NS	NS	NS	NS	NS	NS

measure in favor of the Anglo-American children. Furthermore, there are no sex differences on the capacity measure.

Table 34 contains the ANOVA of the mental age yielded by the Otis-Lennon. In addition to a significant effect of age and one of ethnicity, there is a significant interaction of age with ethnicity. The cell means indicate that among the youngest age group the Mexican-American

TABLE 34. New Mexico grades 4, 5, and 6, Otis-Lennon mental abilities test, mental age: Analysis of variance by age, sex, ethnicity.

	SS	df	MS	F
Age (A)	11.91	2	5.96	20.76***
Sex (B)	.00	1	.00	.00
Ethnicity (C)	1.77	1	1.77	6.18*
A x B	.63	2	.32	1.10
A x C	2.70	2	1.35	4.71**
B x C	.43	1	.43	1.51
A x B x C	.27	2	.14	.47
Within	53.08	185	.29	

*p < .025
**p < .01
***p < .001

children perform better. Table 35 summarizes the ANOVA on the
DIQ. As may be seen, there is a significant effect of ethnicity. Cell
means indicate that the Anglo-American children have higher DIQs
than the Mexican-American children have.

TABLE 35. New Mexico grades 4, 5, and 6, Otis-Lennon mental
abilities test, DIQ: Analysis of variance by age, sex,
ethnicity.

	SS	df	MS	F
Age (A)	80.14	2	40.07	2.47
Sex (B)	.05	1	.05	.00
Ethnicity (C)	70.44	1	70.44	4.35*
A x B	52.94	2	26.47	1.63
A x C	109.47	2	54.73	3.38
B x C	37.39	1	37.39	2.31
A x B x C	.12	2	.06	.00
Within	2997.39	185	16.20	

*p < .05

Examination of the ANOVAs on the CTBS indicates that on the
comprehension scale there is a significant interaction of sex and
ethnic group (see Table 36). In this case, the Anglo males are the
highest scoring of the four sex-ethnic groups. The order of their
performance is as follows: the highest scores are those of the Anglo-
American males, who score better than the Mexican-American females, who in turn score better than the Mexican-American males.
There is a similar sex-ethnic group interaction on the CTBS scale
of verbal expression (Table 37).

TABLE 36. New Mexico grades 4, 5, and 6, CTBS/comprehension:
Analysis of variance by age, sex, ethnicity.

	SS	df	MS	F
Age (A)	170.75	2	85.38	8.75**
Sex (B)	6.05	1	6.05	.62
Ethnicity (C)	22.02	1	22.02	2.26
A x B	5.96	2	2.98	.31
A x C	39.33	2	19.66	2.02
B x C	65.61	1	65.61	6.72*
A x B x C	4.58	2	2.29	.23
Within	1805.34	185	9.76	

*p < .01
**p < .005

TABLE 37. New Mexico grades 4, 5, and 6, CTBS/expression:
Analysis of variance by age, sex, ethnicity.

	SS	df	MS	F
Age (A)	56.96	2	28.48	8.16**
Sex (B)	1.44	1	1.44	.41
Ethnicity (C)	4.53	1	4.53	1.30
A x B	2.65	2	1.33	.38
A x C	13.54	2	6.77	1.94
B x C	19.80	1	19.80	5.68*
A x B x C	5.13	2	2.56	.73
Within	645.47	185	3.49	

*p < .025
**p < .005

Again, the Anglo-American males are the most able performers,
followed by the Mexican-American females, followed by the Anglo-
American females, followed by the Mexican-American males. For
the CTBS scales of arithmetic concepts and arithmetic application,
there is a significant main effect of ethnic group (see Tables 38 and
39). The effect is the same for both of these scales, with the Anglo-
American children performing better than the Mexican-American children.

TABLE 38. New Mexico grades 4, 5, and 6, CTBS/arithmetic
concepts: Analysis of variance by age, sex,
ethnicity.

	SS	df	MS	F
Age (A)	129.68	2	64.84	18.76**
Sex (B)	.18	1	.18	.05
Ethnicity (C)	23.52	1	23.52	6.80*
A x B	11.72	2	5.86	1.70
A x C	16.24	2	8.12	2.35
B x C	5.69	1	5.69	1.65
A x B x C	2.83	2	1.41	.41
Within	639.56	185	3.46	

*p < .01
**p < .001

The total score on the CTBS for grades four, five, and six reflects
both a significant main effect of ethnicity and a significant interaction
of sex and ethnicity (Table 40).

TABLE 39. New Mexico grades 4, 5, and 6, CTBS/arithmetic application: Analysis of variance by age, sex, ethnicity.

	SS	df	MS	F
Age (A)	75.01	2	37.51	18.97**
Sex (B)	1.25	1	1.25	.63
Ethnicity (C)	12.57	1	12.57	6.36*
A x B	10.33	2	5.17	2.61
A x C	4.09	2	2.04	1.03
B x C	1.12	1	1.12	.56
A x B x C	1.13	2	.57	.28
Within	365.83	185	1.98	

*p < .025
**p < .001

TABLE 40. New Mexico grades 4, 5, and 6, CTBS total score.

	SS	df	MS	F
Age (A)	7851.44	2	3925.72	9.96***
Sex (B)	156.29	1	156.29	.40
Ethnicity (C)	1704.12	1	1704.12	4.32*
A x B	194.86	2	97.43	.25
A x C	854.83	2	427.41	1.08
B x C	1649.94	1	1649.94	4.19*
A x B x C	9.30	2	4.65	.01
Within	72911.11	185	394.11	

*p < .05
***p < .001

The main effect of ethnicity indicates that the Anglo-American children score higher than the Mexican-American children. Examination of the ethnicity-sex subgroups indicates that the most superior performances are those of the Anglo-American males, with the two female groups performing at about the same level, and with the Mexican-American males performing the most poorly of all four groups. With respect to the study skills CTBS scale, a significant main effect of ethnicity and a significant sex-ethnicity interaction are again found (Table 41). In general, the Anglo-American children's performance is superior to that of the Mexican-American children. Of the sex-ethnicity groups the Anglo-American males are the highest achievers, with the two female groups following. The Mexican-American males are the lowest achievers of the four groups.

TABLE 41. New Mexico grades 4, 5, and 6, CTBS/study skills
total: Analysis of variance by age, sex, ethnicity.

	SS	df	MS	F
Age (A)	383. 14	2	191. 57	22. 98***
Sex (B)	. 02	1	. 02	. 00
Ethnicity (C)	45. 23	1	45. 23	5. 42**
A x B	54. 78	2	27. 39	3. 28
A x C	30. 65	2	15. 32	1. 84
B x C	33. 63	1	33. 63	4. 03*
A x B x C	. 78	2	. 39	. 05
Within	1542. 44	185	8. 34	

*p < . 05
**p < . 025
***p < . 001

3.2 Colorado

3.2.1 Sample and procedure. The Colorado sample was selected
from children attending three different elementary schools in two
different counties. The Mexican-American children in the sample
comprised 97% of the total. There were three test administrators,
two males and one female, all of whom were bilingual and residents
of the area. The standardized tests were all administered in English,
while the neo-Piagetian measures were administered according to the
language needs of the children. There was no subsampling within the
classroom.

All of the neo-Piagetian measures were administered in the usual
manner. The standardized tests were administered according to
publisher's instructions. The standardized tests administered to the
Colorado children are: California Short Form Test of Mental Maturity
(CTMM-SF) as a measure of capacity, and the California Achievement
Test (CAT) as an achievement measure.

3.2.2 Results. A summary of the Colorado performance on all
measures may be found in Table 42 for grades one, two, and three,
and in Table 43 for grades four, five, and six. It should be noted here
that the CTMM yields several scores which are reported on these
tables: a mental age for the total test, one for the language section,
and one for the non-language section; an IQ based on the results of the
total test, an IQ yielded by the language section, and an IQ yielded by
the non-language section.

TABLE 42. Colorado grades 1, 2, and 3: Performance on developmental, capacity, and achievement measures.

	Grade 1 n=66 Mean	SD	Grade 2 n=56 Mean	SD	Grade 3 n=24 Mean	SD
Chronological age	6-10	-6	7-8	-7	9-1	-7
Developmental measure[a]						
CCS/number (6)	3.88	2.43	4.67	2.18	5.36	1.13
CCS/length (6)	3.76	2.40	4.63	1.91	5.46	1.22
CCS/substance (6)	2.36	2.52	4.08	2.43	5.08	1.47
CCS/space (6)	1.24	1.39	2.29	1.94	2.67	1.95
CCS/weight (6)	1.52	1.87	1.42	1.79	2.75	2.23
WLT/total score (20)	6.82	4.51	9.13	4.18	14.14	3.78
FIT/total score (30)	16.70	7.60	20.88	8.91	21.16	7.84
ST/total score (20)	10.20	2.05	10.71	1.94	11.88	2.17
Capacity measure						
CTMM total mental age	6-10	1-1	7-11	-10	8-7	1-2
CTMM language M.A.	6-10	-8	7-10	1-0	8-11	1-0
CTMM non-language M.A.	7-2	-9	8-0	-9	8-5	1-4
CTMM total IQ	94.62	16.13	93.38	12.79	92.75	13.49
CTMM language IQ	92.65	16.27	96.33	14.54	95.88	11.38
CTMM non-language IQ	97.88	16.49	98.38	11.55	90.58	14.49
Achievement measure[b]						
CAT reading	1.79	.70	2.10	.94	2.69	.67
CAT math	1.58	.59	2.32	.78	3.00	.95
CAT language	1.67	.70	1.97	.78	2.68	.94
CAT spelling	1.57	.58	2.50	.89	2.63	.88
CAT total	1.58	.59	2.15	.76	2.75	.84

Note: Ages expressed in years and months.
[a]Numbers in parentheses represent total number of items in each scale.
[b]Expressed in grade equivalents.

When examining the scores on the developmental measures across the six grades, one must keep in mind that there is a varying percent of overage-per-grade in the six grades and that the six grades are from three different towns. Furthermore, in some cases the sample for a grade involves just one classroom while in others the sample for the grade involves two or three classrooms. Nevertheless, if one examines the scores on the developmental measures across the six grades, a progression reflecting greater mastery of these tasks with age is seen. For example, the mean score for grade one on the CCS/ number scale is 3.88 with a standard deviation of 2.43, whereas the mean score on that same scale for grade six is 5.89 with a much smaller standard deviation of 0.61. In a like manner, the WLT total mean score for grade one is 6.82 with a standard deviation of 4.51,

TABLE 43. Colorado grades 4, 5, and 6: Performance on developmental, capacity, and achievement measures.

	Grade 4 n=20		Grade 5 n=26		Grade 6 n=53	
	Mean	SD	Mean	SD	Mean	SD
Chronological age	9-8	-6	10-11	-9	12-2	-8
Developmental measure[a]						
CCS/number (6)	5.65	.81	5.92	.27	5.89	.64
CCS/length (6)	5.75	.64	5.73	.60	5.85	.63
CCS/substance (6)	5.60	1.19	5.77	.86	5.76	.70
CCS/space (6)	3.80	2.02	3.50	2.06	4.15	1.70
CCS/weight (6)	2.55	2.56	4.35	2.42	2.96	2.54
WLT/total score (20)	15.05	4.37	16.56	3.61	16.41	3.39
FIT/total score (30)	26.80	7.36	28.62	6.17	28.25	7.36
ST/total score (20)	12.10	1.59	13.89	2.27	12.89	2.17
Capacity measure						
CTMM total mental age	10-10	1-2	11-6	1-11	9-11	3-11
CTMM language M.A.	11-0	1-2	11-6	2-0	9-10	3-11
CTMM non-language M.A.	10-8	1-6	11-4	1-8	10-3	4-1
CTMM total IQ	104.90	11.56	99.23	17.23	88.66	18.90
CTMM language IQ	106.30	9.77	100.46	18.11	87.38	19.14
CTMM non-language IQ	103.45	14.81	98.58	14.64	92.38	19.09
Achievement measure[b]						
CAT reading	5.06	.98	5.58	1.71	4.71	1.29
CAT math	4.31	.79	5.26	1.04	5.75	1.09
CAT language	5.21	1.35	5.89	2.00	6.57	1.62
CAT spelling	4.75	1.41	5.64	2.14	6.03	2.10
CAT battery total	4.70	.94	5.47	1.39	5.60	1.14

Note: Ages expressed in years and months.
[a]Expressed in grade equivalents.
[b]Numbers in parentheses represent total number of items in each scale.

whereas the mean score for grade six is 16.41 with a mean score of
3.39.

If one examines Table 42, it may be seen that grades one and two
are generally average with respect to both the capacity and the achievement measures. Further examination of these scores reveals that the
children perform relatively better on the non-language parts of the
capacity measure. On the CAT, it appears both of the grades are
performing at the appropriate level.

The performance of grade three is somewhat different. First, as
may be seen, these children are somewhat old for their grade, the
average age being 9 years and 1 month. (It was found that 16% of the
children in this class were overage for the grade, which would account
for the higher mean age.) Furthermore, it can be seen that their

performance capacity measure is poor. This is perhaps related to the percentage of overage children in that class. The relatively superior performance on the non-language part of the CTMM, present in grades one and two, is not present for this grade. The results for grade three are probably highly biased as all of grade three comes from just one classroom of one school. As the sample selection was left up to the site people, the sampling bias, while it exists, is not defined.

Table 43 presents the performance of grades four, five, and six. The grade four sample is again only one classroom. As seen in the Mental Age and IQ scores, these children, similar to the grade one and grade two children, perform better than average.

The performance of grade five is essentially average to better than average. For example, whereas the mean chronological age is 10 years and 11 months, the mean mental age for the total test is 11 years 6 months, with a standard deviation of 1 year and 11 months. The grade equivalent for the CAT total is 5.47. The grade six results are somewhat aberrant. First, the mean age of 12 years and 2 months is old for this grade and the performance is quite low, i. e. the mental age on the total CTMM is 9 years and 11 months. The consequent IQ scores reflect this discrepancy between chronological age and mental age. It should be noted that 39% of this grade-group is overage for grade. The results on the achievement measure are inconsistent, ranging from a performance of well into the sixth grade on language and spelling, to below the sixth grade in reading, math, and the battery total.

After describing the performance of the Colorado children on both the standardized and developmental measures, it is of interest to examine the interrelation of all of the developmental measures with chronological age and sex. The results of these correlations may be found in Table 44. First, it may be seen that chronological age correlates significantly with all of the developmental measures but not with sex. Secondly, sex does not correlate with any of the developmental measures. Third, all of the developmental measures correlate significantly with each other. There is not one correlation on this part of the matrix which does not attain statistical significance. It may thus be inferred that the developmental measures are in general tapping the same domain.

3. 2. 2. 1 Age and sex differences. The differences within the sample on the developmental and standardized measures according to age and sex were examined. A summary of the results of the age by sex ANOVAs on the developmental measures may be found in Table 45. While there are significant age differences on all the measures which show increased performance with increased age, there are also a few sex differences in performance. These are the total score for the

TABLE 44. Total Colorado sample: Correlations among neo-Piagetian measures (N=226).

	Chrono-logical age	Sex	CCS number	CCS length	CCS substance	CCS space	CCS weight	CCS total	WLT V/H	WLT tilted	WLT 3-D	WLT total	FIT total	ST total
Sex	-.001													
CCS number	.462	-.135												
CCS length	.469	-.092	.742											
CCS substance	.582	-.128	.793	.771										
CCS space	.522	-.098	.292	.292	.403									
CCS weight	.329	-.138	.308	.326	.251	.210								
CCS total	.638	-.160	.826	.823	.886	.588	.612							
WLT V/H	.551	-.086	.455	.378	.495	.392	.258	.529						
WLT tilted	.513	-.234	.264	.280	.337	.486	.254	.440	.469					
WLT 3-D	.650	-.054	.433	.422	.509	.527	.275	.585	.636	.572				
WLT total	.675	-.145	.460	.426	.532	.546	.311	.612	.867	.800	.849			
FIT total	.531	-.024	.414	.354	.490	.443	.241	.520	.481	.463	.524	.579		
ST total	.504	-.060	.400	.352	.453	.360	.317	.507	.334	.316	.378	.405	.391	

TABLE 45. Colorado, all subjects, developmental neo-Piagetian measures: Analysis of variance by age, sex (N=226).

	CCS number	CCS length	CCS substance	CCS space	CCS weight	CCS total	WLT V/H	WLT tilted	WLT 3-D	WLT total	FIT total	ST total
Age	.001	.001	.001	.001	.001	.001	.001	.001	.001	.001	.001	.001
Sex	NS	NS	NS	.05	NS	.05	.05	.001	NS	.001	NS	NS
Age by sex	NS	NS	NS	NS	NS	NS	NS	NS	NS	NS	NS	NS

CCS; the WLT vertical/horizontal bottles score, the WLT tilted bottles score, and the total WLT score. These ANOVAs may be found in Tables 46 through 49. In all of these the direction of the sex differences is the same: males' performance is at a more advanced cognitive level than that of females.

TABLE 46. Colorado, all subjects, CCS total score: Analysis of variance by age, sex.

	SS	df	MS	F
Age (A)	287.10	5	57.42	27.80**
Sex (B)	9.83	1	9.83	4.76*
A x B	11.01	5	2.20	1.07
Within	442.01	214	2.07	

*p < .05
**p < .001

TABLE 47. Colorado, all subjects, WLT, vertical/horizontal bottles: Analysis of variance by age, sex.

	SS	df	MS	F
Age (A)	29.66	5	5.93	19.44**
Sex (B)	1.21	1	1.21	3.97*
A x B	1.14	5	.23	.75
Within	65.29	214	.31	

*p < .05
**p < .001

TABLE 48. Colorado, all subjects, WLT/tilted bottles: Analysis of variance by age, sex.

	SS	df	MS	F
Age (A)	14.36	5	2.87	12.87*
Sex (B)	4.11	1	4.11	18.41*
A x B	.84	5	.17	.75
Within	47.74	214	.22	

*p < .001

TABLE 49. Colorado, all subjects, WLT total score: Analysis of variance by age, sex.

	SS	df	MS	F
Age (A)	159.72	5	31.94	31.69*
Sex (B)	11.62	1	11.62	11.52*
A x B	3.40	5	.68	.67
Within	215.75	214	11.01	

*p < .001

The results of the standardized testing were analyzed in the same way; however, they required analysis of grades one, two, and three individually because different levels of the test were given to them. Grades four, five, and six were analyzed together as they all received the same forms and levels of the two tests. Sex was the only variable examined in grades one through three. The age range was so restricted in each grade that it made no sense to use age as one of the variables.

For grade one there were no sex differences on the CAT. However, on the CTMM, there was a sex difference on both the numerical values scale and on the numerical reasoning scale of the CTMM. Both showed females performing better than males. In grade two there were no sex differences on either test. Grade three, interestingly enough, yielded two scales on which there were sex differences in performance. These are the logical reasoning scale and the non-language raw score of the CTMM. Both of these differences are in the same direction, males performing better than females.

In analyzing grades four, five, and six together, it was possible to use age as one of the variables. The summary of these two-way ANOVAs may be found in Table 50.

With respect to the capacity measure it can be seen that while there was frequently an age main effect, there were no sex differences save for one on the analogy subtest. This effect was in the direction of a higher performance for females. The summary of this particular ANOVA may be found in Table 51. With respect to the achievement test, while there were the expected age differences in performance, there were no sex differences.

TABLE 50. Colorado grades 4, 5, and 6: Analysis of variance by age, sex (N=99).

California Test of Mental Maturity

	Opposites	Similarities	Analogies	Language reasoning	Number reasoning	Number values	Number problems	Number reasoning	Verbal	Memory	Language total	N-lang. total	Total	Language M.A.	Language IQ	N-lang. M.A.	N-lang. IQ	Total M.A.	Total IQ
Age	NS	NS	NS	NS	.001	.001	NS	.01	.001	.025	.025	.01	.01	.05	.001	NS	.025	NS	.001
Sex	NS	NS	.01	NS	NS	NS	NS	NS	NS	NS	NS	NS	NS	NS	NS	NS	NS	NS	NS
Age by sex	NS	NS	.05	NS	NS	NS	NS	NS	NS	NS	NS	NS	NS	NS	NS	NS	NS	NS	NS

California Achievement Tests

	Reading			Math			Language			Spell	Battery
	Vocab.	Compre.	Total	Comput.	Concepts	Total	Mech.	Usage	Total	Spell	Total
Age	.005	.01	.01	.001	.005	.001	.005	NS	.005	NS	.005
Sex	NS	NS	NS	NS	NS	NS	NS	NS	NS	NS	NS
Age by sex	NS	NS	NS	NS	NS	NS	NS	NS	NS	NS	NS

TABLE 51. Colorado grades 4, 5, and 6, California Test of
Mental Maturity, analogies subtest: Analysis of
variance by age, sex.

	SS	df	MS	F
Age (A)	3.39	2	1.69	2.99
Sex (B)	3.15	1	3.15	5.56**
A x B	4.30	2	2.14	3.79*
Within	52.75	93	.57	

   *p < .05
  **p < .01

3.3 Texas

3.3.1 Sample and procedure. The Texas sample was composed of
children from three towns, all within one county in south Texas. Of
the sample, 95% of the children were Mexican-American. The sample
was drawn from six different schools, one school for each grade.
Two classrooms comprised the sample for each grade. There was no
subsampling within the classroom, i.e. all the children in each classroom were used.

Due to the fact that there were three different towns and six different schools involved, it was anticipated that this sample would be an
extremely heterogeneous one. Moreover, which variables would
account for this heterogeneity was not known. The classrooms varied
with respect to the type of program and, therefore, the type of student
found within each classroom. In grades one, three, four, and five,
50% of the children were in the 'migrant program', while in grades
two and four all of the children were in the 'regular' program.

The frequency of Spanish versus English used to administer the
developmental measures also varied from grade to grade. In grade
one, approximately only 15% of the tests were administered in English.
In grade two, approximately 30% of the tests were administered in
English. In grades three and four, approximately 50% of the tests
were administered in English. Approximately 70% of the tests for
grade five were administered in English. In grade six, 90% of the
tests were administered in English.

All of the developmental measures were administered in the con-
ventional manner as described in the first chapter. In grade one all
of the tests were administered individually. In grade two the tests
were generally administered in groups of three. In grade three the
tests tended to be administered in groups of five, whereas in grades
four through six the group size was approximately ten children. The
standardized tests were administered according to the publisher's

instructions, with the groups generally being 25 in number. The standardized tests which were administered are as follows: grades one through six received the appropriate level of the Inter-American Tests of Reading (new series) and grades four, five, and six received in addition the Inter-American Tests of General Ability (new series).

3.3.2 Results. A description of the Texas data with respect to chronological age and performance on capacity, achievement, and developmental measures may be found in Table 52. Close examination of this table shows that the data are not very informative. They do not provide a very clear or conclusive picture with respect to the performance of the Texas children on standardized tests. Examining the chronological age from grade one to grade six, it can be seen that as a whole the sample tends to be overage for grade. In fact, when tabulating overage in grade it was found that 10% of the children in grade one are overage, 45% in grades two and three, 50% in grade four, and 56% in grade five. In grade six, 23% of the children are overage.

If the capacity test scores in Table 52 are examined, it will be seen that no capacity measure was administered to the first three grades, leaving no index of the capacity of these children. In examining the capacity scores for grades four, five, and six, it should be noted that these are total raw scores and are not IQ measures. Therefore, very little can be inferred from them. With respect to the achievement measure it will be seen that only the Inter-American Series Reading Test was administered. As the reading test provides a measure of only reading achievement, one cannot infer the level of achievement of the Texas grades one through six children on any other skill or subject. Furthermore, as with the capacity measure, these scores are raw scores and as such they provide very little information. One cannot even infer relative proficiencies within one grade across the level of reading, speed of reading, and comprehension of reading. Moreover, since these are scores on different levels and forms of the tests, one cannot infer that there is increasing proficiency with increasing scores across grades.

The only data which provide any sort of insight as to the level of performance and capacity of the Texas children are the developmental neo-Piagetian measures. It can be seen that the scores on these measures tend to progress with age, as at the other sites, and that the standard deviation tends to decrease. So, for example, on the CCS/ number scale with a total of six items, the grade one children had a mean score of 3.29 with a standard deviation of 1.86, while the grade six children mastered this task with a mean score of 5.96 and a standard deviation of 0.2. A similar progression in capacity with age can be seen in almost all of the other neo-Piagetian measures. It may thus be said that with respect to developmental progress, the Texas

TABLE 52. Texas grades 1 through 6: Performance on developmental, capacity, and achievement measures.

Measure	Grade 1 N=38 Mean	SD	Grade 2 N=49 Mean	SD	Grade 3 N=44 Mean	SD	Grade 4 N=42 Mean	SD	Grade 5 N=40 Mean	SD	Grade 6 N=47 Mean	SD
Chronological age	6-10	-7	8-3	-10	9-4	-9	10-4	9	11-5	-12	12-1	-7
Developmental measure[a]												
CCS/number (6)	3.29	1.86	4.06	1.66	5.23	1.31	5.78	.61	5.35	1.37	5.96	.20
CCS/length (6)	3.18	2.01	3.80	1.85	4.79	1.72	5.45	1.02	5.15	1.37	5.64	.61
CCS/substance (6)	1.84	1.61	2.76	1.94	4.79	1.84	5.50	1.15	4.90	1.39	5.77	.67
CCS/space (6)	1.82	1.75	1.59	1.62	2.02	1.82	4.17	1.45	3.38	1.92	4.67	1.55
CCS/weight (6)	1.71	1.39	1.73	2.01	2.48	2.26	2.38	2.12	1.70	2.33	2.17	2.28
WLT total (20)	11.75	2.58	10.49	3.60	12.01	2.93	13.34	3.90	12.73	3.91	16.03	2.95
FIT total (30)	23.82	5.39	22.35	6.96	24.04	6.10	25.17	8.38	23.78	7.94	31.23	4.68
ST total (20)	9.60	1.94	11.51	2.01	11.73	2.64	12.50	1.70	12.33	1.90	13.89	2.22
Capacity measure:												
Inter-American General ability total score[b]	--	--	--	--	--	--	82.43	16.69	87.28	22.15	107.66	14.00
Achievement measure:												
Inter-American Reading[c]												
Level	13.05	7.97	17.53	6.54	28.66	5.04	11.26	4.55	18.00	6.40	24.57	6.30
Comprehension	9.95	4.78	14.16	5.01	26.32	5.58	18.12	7.16	20.58	8.95	26.75	7.61
Speed	--	--	5.96	3.54	14.54	5.35	9.69	4.16	14.95	7.04	15.94	4.58

[a]Figure in parentheses is total number of items for scale.
[b]Data not collected for first three age groups.
[c]Only raw scores available.

children appear to be similar to all of the other children in this sample and to other samples of children to whom these developmental measures have been given.

3.3.2.1 Age and sex differences. An objective of the data analysis was age and sex differences within the sample. All of the developmental neo-Piagetian measures were submitted to an age by sex ANOVA. In Table 53 may be seen a summary of all these analyses, indicating which of these yielded significant F's at which level of statistical significance. It may be seen that there are a large number of significant sex differences at this site, more than at any of the other sites. The individual ANOVAs yielding significant sex differences and sex and age interactions may be found in Tables 54 through 60. The direction of the sex differences is the same in all cases, with males performing at more advanced cognitive levels than females. An interesting aspect of the sex differences at this site is that the main effects they produce are very strong, with levels of significance ranging from .05 to .001. At other sites the sex differences were generally at lower levels of significance.

TABLE 53. Texas, all subjects: Summary of analyses of variance, neo-Piagetian measures (N=269).

	CCS number	CCS length	CCS substance	CCS space	CCS weight	CCS total	WLT V/H	WLT tilted	WLT 3-D	WLT total	FIT total	ST total
Age	.001	.001	.001	.001	NS	.001	.025	.001	.001	.001	.001	.001
Sex	.025	NS	.01	NS	NS	.025	.005	.05	NS	.01	.001	NS
Age by sex	.025	NS	NS	NS	NS	NS	NS	NS	NS	NS	NS	NS

TABLE 54. Texas, all subjects, CCS/number: Analysis of variance by age, sex (N=269).

	SS	df	MS	F
Age (A)	10.51	5	2.10	23.99**
Sex (B)	.47	1	.47	5.31*
A x B	1.22	5	.24	2.79*
Within	22.52	257	.09	

*p < .025
**p < .001

TABLE 55. Texas, all subjects, CCS/substance: Analysis of variance by age, sex (N=269).

	SS	df	MS	F
Age (A)	24.58	5	4.92	40.47**
Sex (B)	.84	1	.84	6.94*
A x B	.99	5	.20	1.62
Within	31.22	257	.12	

*p < .01
**p < .001

TABLE 56. Texas, all subjects, CCS total scores: Analysis of variance by age, sex (N=269).

	SS	df	MS	F
Age (A)	226.17	5	45.23	31.04**
Sex (B)	8.44	1	8.44	5.79*
A x B	8.39	5	1.68	1.15
Within	374.56	257	1.46	

*p < .025
**p < .001

TABLE 57. Texas, all subjects, WLT, vertical/horizontal: Analysis of variance by age, sex (N=269).

	SS	df	MS	F
Age (A)	2.31	5	.46	2.98*
Sex (B)	1.44	1	1.44	9.27**
A x B	1.67	5	.34	2.15
Within	39.86	257	.16	

*p < .025
**p < .005

TABLE 58. Texas, all subjects, WLT/tilted bottles: Analysis of variance by age, sex (N=269).

	SS	df	MS	F
Age (A)	5.83	5	1.17	7.23**
Sex (B)	.64	1	.64	3.96*
A x B	.49	5	.10	.61
Within	41.44	257	.16	

*p < .05
**p < .001

TABLE 59. Texas, all subjects, WLT total score: Analysis of variance by age, sex (N=269).

	SS	df	MS	F
Age (A)	26.48	5	5.30	9.10**
Sex (B)	4.53	1	4.53	7.79*
A x B	2.60	5	.52	.89
Within	149.61	257	.58	

*p < .01
**p < .001

TABLE 60. Texas, all subjects, FIT total score: Analysis of variance by age, sex (N=269).

	SS	df	MS	F
Age (A)	58.17	5	11.63	5.05*
Sex (B)	26.25	1	26.25	11.40*
A x B	10.84	5	2.17	.94
Within	591.63	257	2.30	

*p < .001

TABLE 61. Texas, all subjects, Inter-American Test: Analysis of variance by age, sex.

Test of Reading, Level 2, Form DE, Grades 2, 3				
	Comprehension			
	Level	Speed	Vocabulary	Total
Age	.005	.001	.005	.001
Sex	NS	.01	NS	NS
Age by sex	NS	NS	.05	NS
Test of Reading, Level 3, Form DE, grades 4, 5, 6				
	Comprehension			
	Level	Speed	Vocabulary	Total
Age	.001	.001	.001	.001
Sex	NS	NS	NS	NS
Age by sex	NS	NS	NS	NS

Test of General Ability, Form CE, Grades 4, 5, 6 (N=143)						
	Sentence	Analogies	Computation	Word relations	Classifications	Series	Total
Age	.001	NS	.001	NS	NS	NS	NS
Sex	NS	NS	NS	NS	NS	NS	NS
Age by sex	NS	NS	NS	NS	NS	NS	NS

There were age by sex ANOVAs also computed on the standardized tests, the Inter-American Series. Those grades which received the same levels and forms of tests were analyzed together. Grade one showed no sex differences on the reading tests. The results of grades two through six may be found in Table 61. For grades two and three, it may be seen that there is a strong effect of sex on speed of (reading) comprehension and an interaction of age and sex on the vocabulary scale. It may be seen in the lower two-thirds of the table that there are no further sex differences in this sample.

The summary data for the two ANOVAs on grades two and three may be found in Tables 62 and 63. The differences on speed of comprehension indicate that females perform better than do males on this scale. With respect to the vocabulary scale and the age by sex interaction, in the younger age group the males do better than the females, while in the older age group the females do better than the males. Rank-ordering all four of these age-sex groups gives us the following order: the best performance is found in the older females, followed by the older males, followed by the younger males, followed by the younger females.

TABLE 62. Texas grades 2 and 3, Inter-American Test of Reading/speed of comprehension: Analysis of variance by age, sex.

	SS	df	MS	F
Age (A)	22.42	1	22.42	13.03**
Sex (B)	13.05	1	13.05	7.58*
A x B	.19	1	.19	.11
Within	154.88	90	1.72	

*p < .01
**p < .001

TABLE 63. Texas grades 2 and 3, Inter-American Test of Reading/vocabulary: Analysis of variance by age, sex.

	SS	df	MS	F
Age (A)	30.17	1	30.17	9.66**
Sex (B)	.00	1	.00	.00
A x B	14.55	1	14.55	4.66*
Within	281.11	90	3.12	

*p < .05
**p < .005

In general summary of the data on the Texas sample, it can be said that there are not enough data to provide any clarity or any description of the Texas sample with respect to anything other than the developmental measures. As previously mentioned, the developmental measures indicate that these children are performing in a manner comparable to the children at all of the other sites.

3.4 California

3.4.1 Sample and procedure. The sampling procedure and instrument administration at this site differed from those at the other sites in several ways. The sample consisted primarily of monolingual Spanish children who are from families in the agricultural migrant stream. All these children were at the California site for a particular agricultural season. Contrary to the procedure utilized in the past, there was subsampling within the classroom, i.e. migrant children were taken from their monolingual English classrooms and tested separately. The migrant children came from ten different elementary schools within the district. All of the tests were administered, of necessity, in Spanish by three test administrators, two males and one female, all of whom are bilingual and are from the area. Ninety-eight percent of the children were Spanish surnamed.

All of the developmental neo-Piagetian measures were administered either individually or in small groups, with the size of the group depending on the specific circumstances. The only standardized capacity or achievement measure which it was possible to administer was a Spanish translation of the Peabody Picture Vocabulary Test (PPVT). This test yields a score which is an indicator of vocabulary IQ. As these children are part of the migrant stream and are not considered an actual part of the school district, they received no district-administered achievement measures, nor were scores from any previous administrations available. The PPVT was administered by the site personnel and it is not a part of any routine school district testing. Furthermore, as the children were generally monolingual Spanish speakers and were in classrooms throughout the school system which utilized only the English language, there was no standardized achievement measure which could be used. The PPVT appeared to be the only measure of achievement (or capacity) usable.

3.4.2 Results. The results of the testing will be first described in terms of the means and standard deviations of the various scores for children of all six grades. Following that, a presentation of the intercorrelations of the developmental neo-Piagetian measures with the PPVT will be presented. Then, the age and sex differences within the sample will be discussed.

3.4.2.1 Description of sample. Table 64 contains the mean and standard deviations for all six grades on the following measures: chronological age, PPVT mental age, PPVT IQ, and all of the neo-Piagetian measures.

As may be seen by examining the chronological age, the sample as a whole tends to be overage for grade. This in combination with a somewhat low score on the PPVT mental age yields a vocabulary IQ for grades one through five of less than average. As may be seen, the IQ grade six is slightly greater than average.

In marked contrast to this performance on the Spanish PPVT is the sample's performance on the developmental neo-Piagetian measures. As may be seen by examining Table 64, the sample has readily grasped the first three neo-Piagetian concepts: number, length, and substance. Furthermore, the sixth graders have mastered the concept of space. The relative difficulty of the weight concept that is apparent here is also seen at the other three sites. The expected level of performance on the WLT, the FIT, and ST, was attained by the California sample. As may be seen, there is progressive mastery of these three tasks with age. For example, the mean FIT total score for grade one was 16.89 with a standard deviation of 8.69, while for grade six the mean was 30.14 with a standard deviation of 6.03.

In Table 65 may be seen the relationship of the developmental neo-Piagetian measures to the three scores yielded by the PPVT in conjunction with chronological age and sex. This matrix contains some interesting relationships. First, all of the measures are positively correlated with chronological age as expected. Second, in examining the correlations with sex, it may be seen that sex is not related to any of the developmental measures or to the PPVT. Third, the CCS weight scale is not related to any other measure. This result is not unusual, for the weight scale was not mastered by any age group within this sample and therefore the variance of the scores is highly restricted. This restricted variance suppresses the correlation. Fourth, the ST does not tend to correlate with many of the other measures. Again, this is probably accounted for by a lack of variance. Examination of the mean scores across grades indicates that all grades have mastered this task, thus the limited variance. Fifth, the PPVT IQ score does not correlate with any of the developmental measures. This finding is of interest and of theoretical importance. Moreover, PPVT raw score and the PPVT mental age have few significant correlations with the developmental measures, although their lack of relationship to developmental measures is by no means as great as the PPVT IQ score. The highest correlation of the PPVT mental age score with any of the developmental measures is with the total score on the WLT. The second highest correlation is with the total score on the FIT.

TABLE 64. California grades 1 through 6: Performance on developmental measures and Peabody Picture Vocabulary.

	Grade 1 N=64		Grade 2 N=62		Grade 3 N=46		Grade 4 N=52		Grade 5 N=41		Grade 6 N=22	
	Mean	SD	Mean	SD	Mean	SD	Mean	SD	Mean	SD	Mean	SD
Chronological age (years)	7-3	-8	8-6	-11	9-6	-7	10-9	-9	11-7	-9	12-8	-8
Developmental measure[a]												
CCS number (6)	4.83	1.64	5.53	1.24	5.93	0.33	5.88	0.38	5.80	0.60	5.91	0.29
CCS length (6)	5.02	1.34	5.37	1.40	5.64	0.68	5.90	0.36	5.85	0.36	5.77	0.87
CCS substance (6)	4.00	2.06	4.87	1.66	5.41	1.28	5.58	0.87	5.61	1.09	5.95	0.21
CCS space (6)	1.72	1.61	1.83	1.79	2.50	1.89	3.56	2.10	3.73	1.90	4.04	2.01
CCS weight (6)	0.75	1.11	2.02	2.24	1.91	1.86	2.36	2.43	2.85	2.29	2.73	2.66
WLT total (20)	9.64	4.25	11.19	3.53	12.53	3.02	14.69	3.57	15.46	3.00	16.03	2.66
FIT total (30)	16.89	8.69	21.85	7.50	25.48	7.37	29.02	5.49	28.46	6.82	30.14	6.03
ST total (20)	11.52	3.45	11.25	2.19	12.07	1.81	12.71	1.98	13.05	2.35	12.86	2.01
PPVT mental age[b]	6-10	2-2	7-7	1-10	9-4	2-10	10-7	1-1	10-7	3-0	13-5	3-9
PPVT IQ	92.81	16.11	89.68	17.42	96.02	19.73	96.14	22.84	91.71	19.91	104.75	23.84

a Figures in parentheses are total number of items for scale.

b In years and months.

TABLE 65. California: Correlations among PPVT and neo-Piagetian measures (N=274).

	Chrono-logical age	Sex	CCS number	CCS length	CCS substance	CCS space	CCS weight	WLT total	FIT total	ST total	PPVT IQ	PPVT raw score
Sex	.010											
CCS number	.279	.027										
CCS length	.264	.031	.660									
CCS substance	.349	-.039	.649	.644								
CCS space	.396	-.098	.201	.153	.257							
CCS weight	.263	-.056	.089	.100	.122	.120						
WLT total	.536	-.102	.382	.368	.389	.422	.171					
FIT total	.510	.002	.378	.427	.490	.381	.094	.606				
ST total	.222	.044	.157	.147	.165	.166	.081	.222	.277			
PPVT IQ	.113	.018	.092	.032	.146	.165	-.047	.150	.170	.158		
PPVT raw score	.619	.052	.221	.162	.296	.338	.098	.407	.402	.234	.819	
PPVT mental age	.622	.043	.232	.173	.310	.359	.107	.414	.405	.234	.827	.984

$p < .05$, $r = .195$

$p < .01$, $r = .254$

$p < .001$, $r = .321$

3.4.2.2 Age and sex differences. In addition to the performance of
the sample on the developmental neo-Piagetian measures and on the
PPVT, possible age and sex differences were of interest. In examining the data for such differences, a series of age by sex ANOVAs on
the developmental neo-Piagetian measures were calculated. These
may be found in Table 66. As may be seen, all of the developmental
measures yielded age differences which empirically bear out a theoretically important difference. Second, it may be seen that there are
few sex differences. There is a sex difference on the CCS/space, on
the WLT vertical/horizontal bottle scale, and on the WLT total score.
The sex differences are all in the same direction, that is, males perform at a more advanced cognitive level than females. There was a
significant interaction of age and sex found on the CCS/weight scale.
The age-sex group means indicate that males tended to perform at
higher levels than females except for the second-youngest age group
and the fourth-youngest age group, where the females performed at
a more advanced level than the males. The specific summary of
these ANOVAs may be found in Tables 67 through 70.

TABLE 66. California neo-Piagetian tests: Analysis of variance by age, sex (N=283).

	CCS number	CCS length	CCS substance	CCS space	CCS weight	CCS total	WLT V/H	WLT tilted	WLT total	FIT	ST
Age	.001	.001	.001	.001	.001	.001	.001	.001	.001	.001	.005
Sex	NS	NS	NS	.025*	NS	NS	.025*	NS	.025*	NS	NS
Age by sex	NS	NS	NS	NS	.025	NS	NS	NS	NS	NS	NS

TABLE 67. California, all subjects, CCS/space: Analysis of
variance by age, sex.

	SS	df	MS	F
Age (A)	7.69	5	1.54	9.77**
Sex (B)	.81	1	.81	5.12*
A x B	.50	5	.10	.63
Within	42.72	271	.16	

*p < .025
**p < .001

TABLE 68. California, all subjects, CCS/weight: Analysis of variance by age, sex.

	SS	df	MS	F
Age (A)	5.33	5	1.066	5.84**
Sex (B)	.30	1	.30	1.66
A x B	2.59	5	.52	2.84*
Within	49.44	271	.18	

*p < .025
**p < .001

TABLE 69. California, all subjects, WLT vertical/horizontal bottles: Analysis of variance by age, sex.

	SS	df	MS	F
Age (A)	8.71	5	1.74	11.78**
Sex (B)	.89	1	.89	6.02*
A x B	.31	5	.06	.41
Within	40.09	271	.15	

*p < .025
**p < .001

TABLE 70. California, all subjects, WLT total score: Analysis of variance by age, sex.

	SS	df	MS	F
Age (A)	58.84	5	11.77	21.44**
Sex (B)	2.77	1	2.77	5.05*
A x B	.64	5	.13	.23
Within	148.73	271	.55	

*p < .025
**p < .001

TABLE 71. California, two-way analysis of variance by age, sex, Peabody picture vocabulary test (N=282).

	IQ	Mental age
A (Age)	NS	.001
B (Sex)	NS	NS
AB (Age/Sex)	NS	NS

Age by sex ANOVAs were also calculated on the PPVT. The results of these may be found in Table 71. As may be seen, PPVT IQ showed no difference along the age or sex variables and PPVT mental age showed a main effect of age significant at the .001 level.

CHAPTER 4

COMPARATIVE ANALYSES OF DATA

A natural consequence of examining the performance of each site individually was to compare the sites with one another. It was felt that the sites were different enough in terms of social, economic, political, and demographic variables to affect some performance differences. Attempts were made to collect and synthesize objective, quantifiable data to reflect these perceived site differences before actually comparing site performance data. The collection of such data, however, proved to be problematic. While an attempt was made to obtain demographic and SES-type data from the sites and also to utilize 1970 census data, neither approach was successful. The first approach was unsuccessful because it was impossible to have the sites provide appropriate data. The second approach, a utilization of the census data, was also not possible for the geographic units reflected by the school samples did not coincide with the enumerated units in the census. For example, the Colorado sample was from a school district covering certain areas of two counties while the census data are recorded by counties only. Furthermore, the populations represented by the samples--e. g. migrant families at the California site--are not necessarily represented at all in the census enumeration. For these reasons, it was difficult to reflect specific quantifiable SES and demographic differences between the sites and to use these either to predict or to account for any site score differences.

Nevertheless, it is important to attempt to impart some of the distinguishing characteristics of the sites as these differences color a researcher's perception and interpretation of the quantifiable data. These characteristics will be presented in much the same manner as the researchers encountered them.

65

4.1 New Mexico. The New Mexico sample represents the most middle-class group within the total sample. The sample, drawn from a single elementary school, represents a population primarily from one suburban development outside a central urban area. It is classified as urban by the census. While there are children in the sample whose families receive welfare assistance, there are also Mexican-American children whose parents are professionals and are in state-level politics. The population from which these children are drawn is basically stable. Furthermore, it is the most assimilated with respect to language; none of the tests were administered in Spanish. The data are very complete as the capacity and achievement tests are part of the statewide testing program. They are also of good quality, especially the neo-Piagetian, as the site administrators here were the most experienced with children of this age of all of the four state site personnel. Furthermore, the New Mexico school district was extremely cooperative in the entire testing effort.

4.2 Colorado. Both of the counties from which the three schools comprising the sample were drawn are classified by the 1970 census as rural, non-farm, and are quite poor. Each of the counties have populations of less than 5,000 people. The three schools comprising the sample each contributed two grades. How the three specific schools were selected or how it was decided which school would contribute which grade is not known.

Although the per capita income of these two counties tends to be quite low, the percentage of school-age children enrolled in school is very high. This sample, like the New Mexico one, tends to be very stable. There was no indication that these areas are heavily involved in agricultural crop production, nor that any of the children in the sample are part of the migrant stream.

4.3 Texas. As previously indicated, the results of the Texas testing were inconclusive and in some cases extremely aberrant. It therefore becomes important to speak to these circumstances. It should be remembered that the Texas sample was drawn from three different towns and six different schools. The motivation for these selections remains with the site personnel. The Mexican-American population of this three-town area of southern Texas appears to have three general components: those who have lived in this area for many years or even generations, and whose livelihood is not dependent on seasonal migration; those who are a regular part of the seasonal agricultural migration, i.e. migrant laborers; and recent immigrants from Mexico (who may or may not be migrant laborers). Thus, a sizable number of the school population of this area at any one time may be considered to be newcomers, and not to have the advantages of a consistent curriculum and teaching staff.

With respect to this particular sample, it is known that 50% of the children in grades one, three, four, and five were in an unspecified 'migrant' program. In addition, approximately 50% of the children in grades two, three, four, and five were overage for their grade. Thus, it may be seen that the performance of this Texas sample was subjected to many diverse and adverse influences.

To speak further to the issue of adverse effects on the Texas sample's performance, it should be noted that the tests which were administered in addition to the neo-Piagetian measures, the Inter-American Series, were chosen and administered by site personnel. As mentioned previously, this administration was not complete: with respect to achievement, only reading achievement was assessed and there was no capacity measure administered to grades one through three. Furthermore, site personnel were not trained in the administration of these latter tests by the project.

4.4 California. This sample is similar to the Texas sample in that it is an unusual one. Comprising children all from migrant families within a single school district, it is easily seen to be quite separate from the school district population as a whole. Since the sample is almost entirely monolingual Spanish-speaking, it constitutes the extreme end of a continuum with respect to language assimilation, with the New Mexico sample falling at the extreme other end. This sample is also similar to the Texas one in the large number of children overage for grade. In grades two through six, 40-60% of the children are overage for their grade.

This sample is also unusual because it was not possible to assess its achievement in school-related subjects due to the lack of achievement tests appropriate for Spanish-speaking children and due to the lack of records on previous testing. Also, the question of achievement in school-related skills is a highly problematic one because these children are migrants and though they speak little or no English, they were placed throughout the school district in monolingual English-speaking classes.

4.5 Overage for grade. One attempt at quantifying some of the existing differences between sites was an analysis of the percentage of children in a grade who are overage for that grade. These data provide some basis of comparison of the sites and in some sense provide material for inferences to be drawn about differences between sites. As may be seen in Table 72, each grade at each site was analyzed in terms of the extent to which the children in the samples

TABLE 72. Number of students out of grade by age.

Grade	Total N for grade	Number underage	% underage	Number overage	% overage
New Mexico					
Grade 1	55	0	0	0	0
Grade 2	58	12	21	5	9
Grade 3	80	8	10	14	18
Grade 4	73	10	14	7	10
Grade 5	63	4	6	6	10
Grade 6	73	6	8	7	10
					Avg. 9.5
Colorado					
Grade 1	74	0	0	8	11
Grade 2	26	4	15	3	12
Grade 3	25	0	0	4	16
Grade 4	20	0	0	2	10
Grade 5	27	0	0	8	30
Grade 6	54	3	6	21	39
					Avg. 21
Texas					
Grade 1	40	0	0	4	10
Grade 2	49	0	0	22	45
Grade 3	47	1	2	21	45
Grade 4	44	0	0	22	50
Grade 5	41	2	5	23	56
Grade 6	48	0	0	11	23
					Avg. 38
California					
Grade 1	64	6	9	16	25
Grade 2	60	3	5	24	40
Grade 3	44	2	5	18	41
Grade 4	52	2	4	25	48
Grade 5	41	3	7	22	54
Grade 6	22	1	5	11	50
					Avg. 42

in that grade were either overage or underage with respect to the expected age range for that grade.

The extent of overageness at the New Mexico site in the first grade is 0, whereas in the sixth grade it is approximately 10%. The average overageness across the six grades is about 9.5%. At Colorado a slight increase in overageness can be seen, with a general progression across grades. In the first grade, 11% of the children are overage, while 39% of the sixth graders are overage. On the average across the six grades, approximately 21% of the children are too old for the grade in which they are placed. Turning to the Texas site, a some- what more extreme picture emerges. While only 10% of the children in the first grade are overage, the overageness jumps to 45% for the second and third grades and 50 and 56% for the fourth and fifth grades. In the sixth grade the percentage drops back appreciably to 23%. Thus, an average of 38% of the children in the entire Texas sample were be- low their appropriate grade level. The California percentages are as high as those in Texas and are in some cases higher. As may be seen, 25% of the first graders are overage for grade. The average across all grades is 42% overage.

4.6 Comparison of neo-Piagetian performance data. These descriptions of the differences of the sites and the overageness data may be properly used as a background from which to compare differ- ences in performance on the neo-Piagetian measures. No other mea- sures were compared, as the intelligence and achievement measures varied by site. The first analysis of the neo-Piagetian data consists of examining site-by-site differences. The second comparison of the four sites is made on the basis of sex differences.

4.6.1 Site differences in performance. Initial examination con- sisted of plotting the performance scores on the neo-Piagetian mea- sures for each site as a function of chronological age. The plot of the CCS may be found in Figure 4. As may be seen, there is a high degree of similarity of performance across the four sites. The similarity is greatest for the three oldest age groups.

FIGURE 4. Conservation Scales mean total scores (raw), all sites.

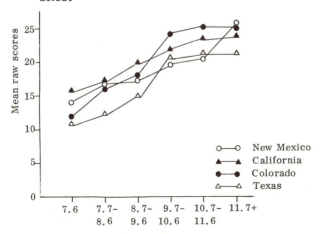

Figure 5 provides a summary of performance for the four sites across age on the WLT. With the exception of the Texas site, there is again a high degree of similarity of performance across sites and greater similarity for the three oldest age groups. Although the performance levels at the Texas site are not exceedingly different from the other sites, it is the failure to find an increase in performance with age that makes it different from the other three sites. Figures 6 and 7 show the performance curves for the FIT and the ST. As in the case of the CCS and the WLT, there is a high degree of consistency across the four sites. Again, with the exception of Texas, performance on all of the tests is linearly related to age.

FIGURE 5. Water Level Task mean total scores (raw), all sites.

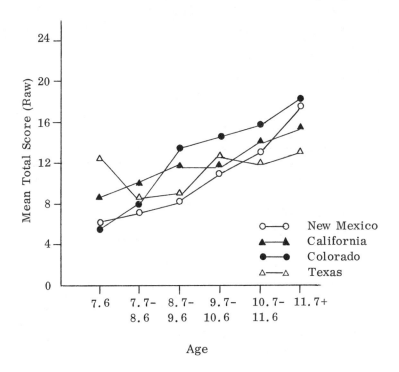

Age

Thus, for each measure the performance across the sites seems to be very similar, with no apparent differences between sites except for Texas. The Texas data seem somewhat aberrant due to there being a failure in achieving a linear relationship with age.

Whether there was any statistical significance in performance across sites was tested in a series of three-way ANOVAs where age, sex, and site were used as the independent variables. The results of

FIGURE 6. Figure Intersection Scales mean total scores (raw), all sites.

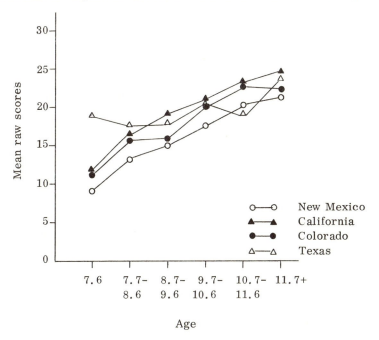

FIGURE 7. Serial Task mean total score (raw), all sites.

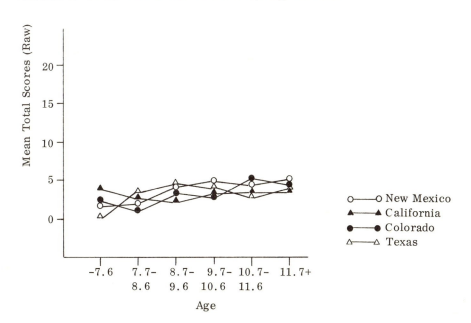

TABLE 73. Total sample, developmental neo-Piagetian measures: Analysis of variance by age, sex, site.

	CCS number	CCS length	CCS substance	CCS space	CCS weight	CCS total	WLT V/H	WLT tilt	WLT 3-D	WLT total	FIT	ST
Age (A)	.001	.001	.001	.001	.001	.001	.001	.001	.001	.001	.001	.001
Sex (B)	.01	NS	.01	.001	.025	.001	.001	.001	.05	.001	.001	NS
Site	.001	.001	.001	NS	.005	.001	.001	.001	.001	.001	.001	NS
A x B	.05	NS	NS	NS	NS	NS	NS	NS	NS	NS	NS	NS
A x C	.001	.001	.001	.05	.005	.001	.001	.001	NS	.001	.001	.001
B x C	NS	NS	NS	NS	NS	NS	NS	.01	NS	NS	NS	NS
A x B x C	NS	NS	NS	NS	NS	NS	NS	NS	NS	NS	NS	NS

these analyses are summarized in Table 73. As may be seen, in addition to significant main effects for age on each test, there were many significant main effects for site. In addition, there are many age by site interactions that are statistically significant. These latter were not anticipated.

In order to examine more comprehensively the main effect of site and the interaction of age and site, an analysis of covariance was employed. This procedure with age as a covariate would statistically correct for age differences of the children at the sites. The results of this analysis are provided in Table 74. As may be seen, the adjusted means still result in statistically significant differences between sites.

TABLE 74. Total sample, neo-Piagetian measures total scores: Analysis of covariance by site, age as covariate (total sample mean age = 9.722).

	New Mexico N=402 A	Colorado N=226 B	Texas N=269 C	California N=283 D	F
Mean age (years)	9.643	9.587	10.128	9.588	
Mean CCS total score	19.677	19.221	18.851	20.806	5.37
Adjusted mean CCS total score	19.831	19.482	18.068	21.123	p < .005
Mean WLT total score	11.454	12.042	12.741	12.688	21.48
Adjusted mean WLT total score	11.567	12.233	12.167	12.921	p < .001
Mean FIT total score	21.112	22.394	25.052	24.212	8.21
Adjusted mean FIT total score	21.282	22.682	24.187	24.562	p < .001
Mean ST total score	11.881	11.664	11.948	12.092	8.60
Adjusted mean ST total score	11.926	11.740	11.720	12.184	p < .001

Several Newman-Keuls post hoc comparisons of ANOVA cell means were then performed to ascertain where the differences between sites lay. None of the differences between means as established by the Newman-Keuls procedure were significant, i.e. no difference between any two sites was found to be statistically significant. Such an occurrence is not unusual and an explanation of it may be found in Hays (1963). Basically, it means that one true comparison among all those possible is significant, but that the researcher will not necessarily find it in his current body of data.

These circumstances caused an examination of the absolute differences of the site mean scores. These may be found in Table 75. It may be seen by inspecting this table that these differences are exceedingly small. For example, the difference between mean scores for New Mexico and Texas on the CCS total score is only 0.83 points out

TABLE 75. Absolute difference in points of adjusted-for-age means on neo-Piagetian measures.

	New Mexico Texas	New Mexico Colorado	New Mexico California	Texas Colorado	Texas California	Colorado California	SD of test
CCS total score (30)	.83	.46	1.13	.37	1.95	1.58	6.60
WLT total score (20)	1.29	.59	1.23	.70	.05	.65	4.82
FIT total score (32)	3.95	1.28	3.10	2.66	.84	1.82	7.72
ST total score (20)	.07	.22	.21	.28	.14	.43	2.32

Note: Numbers in parentheses indicate total number of points possible.

of a possible 30 points, where the standard deviation is 6.60 points. The lack of magnitude of the absolute differences between sites, viewed in conjunction with the failure to find significant differences with the use of the Newman-Keuls post hoc comparison procedure, leads to the position that the present body of data does not contain sufficient evidence to say that the sites are different in their performance.

4.6.2 Sex differences in performance. The circumstances surrounding the presence of sex differences at the sites are similar in nature to the site differences. As shown in Table 76 the three-way ANOVAS resulted in many sex differences which would indicate that the sex variable has a much greater influence in performance than would have been predicted from theory. As it was felt that three-way ANOVAs might be too powerful a test, the two-way ANOVAs performed for each site were reexamined. They were consolidated and may be found in Table 76. As may be seen, sex still has some importance but not to the same extent as would be inferred from examining the three-way ANOVAs.

In order to ascertain more clearly the nature and extent of the sex differences, an analysis of covariance by sex on total scores of the neo-Piagetian measures was conducted. Age was used as a covariant in order to control for age differences between the sexes. The results of this analysis are summarized in Table 77. It may be seen that the analysis yielded a most interesting finding. The significant main effect of sex found on total scores on all the neo-Piagetian measures does not occur when a correction is made for age. In other words, the correction of the age discrepancy by statistical procedures eliminated the sex differences on the neo-Piagetian total scores.

Another analysis of covariance by sex, using age as the covariant, was performed on scores of individual subscales of the CCS. These results may be found in Table 78. In contrast to the previous results, the difference in age between the sexes when corrected by the analysis of covariance does not eliminate the difference in performance on three CCS subscales: number, length, and substance. What this means is that a correction of the age difference between the sexes does not eliminate all of the sex differences in performance. It

TABLE 76. Developmental neo-Piagetian measures: Two-way analysis of variance, age by sex.

	CCS number	CCS length	CCS substance	CCS space	CCS weight	CCS total	WLT V/H	WLT Tilted	WLT 3-D	WLT total	FTT	ST
Total sample												
Age (A)	.001	.001	.001	.001	.001	.001	.001	.001	.001	.001	.001	.001
Sex (B)	.025	NS	.005	.001	.01	.001	.001	.001	.05	.001	.001	NS
AB	.05	NS	.05	NS	NS	NS	NS	NS	NS	NS	NS	NS
New Mexico												
Age (A)	.001	.001	.001	.001	.001	.001	.001	.001	.001	.001	.001	.001
Sex (B)	NS	NS	NS	.001	NS	NS	NS	.05	NS	.025	.005	NS
AB	NS	NS	NS	NS	NS	NS	.025	NS	NS	NS	NS	NS
Colorado												
Age (A)	.001	.001	.001	.001	.001	.001	.001	.001	.001	.001	.001	.001
Sex (B)	NS	NS	.01	NS	NS	.05	.05	.001	NS	.001	NS	NS
AB	NS	NS	NS	NS	NS	NS	NS	NS	NS	NS	NS	NS
Texas												
Age (A)	.001	.001	.001	.001	NS	.001	.025	.001	.001	.001	.001	.001
Sex (B)	.025	NS	NS	NS	NS	.025	.005	.05	NS	.01	.001	NS
AB	.025	NS	NS	NS	NS	NS	NS	NS	NS	NS	NS	NS
California												
Age (A)	.001	.001	.001	.005	.001	.001	.001	.001	.001	.001	.001	.005
Sex (B)	NS	NS	NS	.025	NS	NS	.025	NS	.05	.025	NS	NS
AB	NS	NS	NS	NS	.025	NS	NS	NS	NS	NS	NS	NS

TABLE 77. Total sample, developmental neo-Piagetian measures total scores: Analysis of covariance by sex, age as covariate (total sample mean age = 9.722).

	Males N=587	Females N=593	F
Mean age (years)	9.729	9.716	
Mean CCS total score	20.392	18.960	2.36 NS
Adjusted mean score	20.379	18.972	
Mean WLT total score	12.728	11.590	.20 NS
Adjusted mean score	12.718	11.600	
Mean FIT total score	23.727	22.278	1.41 NS
Adjusted mean score	23.713	22.293	
Mean ST total score	11.876	11.934	3.10 NS
Adjusted mean score	11.872	11.938	

TABLE 78. Total sample, CCS scale scores: Analysis of covariance by sex, age as covariate (total sample mean age = 9.722).

	Males N=587	Females N=593	F
Mean age	9.729	9.716	--
Mean number score	5.310	5.099	6.362
Adjusted mean score	5.308	5.102	p < .025
Mean length score	5.065	4.975	4.453
Adjusted mean score	5.063	4.977	p < .05
Mean substance score	4.729	4.425	6.209
Adjusted mean score	4.726	4.428	p < .025
Mean space score	3.095	2.619	.003 NS
Adjusted space score	3.092	2.622	
Mean weight score	2.193	1.841	1.656 NS
Adjusted weight score	2.191	1.843	

should be noted, however, that as with the site differences, the absolute sex differences are very small. Therefore, rather than be taken as evidence for sex differences on these three conservation concepts, these data more properly serve as stimulation and direction for further investigation.

4.6.3 Field independence and WLT. The issue with respect to field independence-field dependence is based on the findings of Ramirez (1972) and Saarni (1973), which were discussed in the introduction. The question is whether the current data replicate these findings: (1) Mexican-American children are more field dependent than Anglo-American children, and (2) females are more field dependent than males. If such results are obtained, then the question becomes whether these differences are associated with a less able cognitive performance for the field dependent group.

The data relevant to the ethnicity-field dependence relationship are found in the New Mexico data. Age by sex by ethnicity ANOVAs were calculated on the three subscales of the WLT and on the total score. There were no significant main effects for ethnicity. With respect to sex, there were, however, significant main effects on the WLT total score (p < .05) and on the WLT tilted bottles scale (p < .05). Both significant effects are in the direction of males being more field independent.

The sex data for the entire sample are in agreement with the New Mexico data. There are significant main effects for sex on all three of the WLT subscales on the Total Score (p < .001).

An analysis of covariance by sex was also performed on these data, with age as the covariate. It was performed because it was noticed that the females were consistently younger than the males. The results of the analysis of covariance were reported on Table 18. It should be recalled that once the effect of age on sex differences was controlled for all, sex differences in total scores failed to occur, the WLT total score included. This finding negates both the sex-related field dependence finding and the question of whether field dependence is associated with less advanced cognitive performance. Furthermore, examination of the standardized capacity and achievement data site by site reveals no systematic or consistent sex difference in performance.

4.6.4 Ethnic group differences in performance. Since the study was designed to describe Mexican-American children rather than compare them to Anglo-American children, ethnic group comparisons were not built into the study and site personnel were not requested to make certain they obtained a certain number of Anglo-American children. The result was that only at the New Mexico site were there enough Anglo-American children to make it possible to examine ethnic group differences. It will be recalled that there emerged no ethnic group differences on the developmental neo-Piagetian measures, but that there were many consistent ones on the standardized capacity and achievement measures.

The following data bear out the failure to find ethnic group differences on the developmental measures. They consist of data generated by the CCS by an Anglo-American sample. The sample was obtained in Boulder, Colorado (see De Avila and Phyphers 1968). The data from this sample are plotted in Figure 8, along with the corresponding data from the sample currently under study.

FIGURE 8. Comparison of Anglo- and Mexican-American populations, Conservation of Substance (CCS), probability of correct response.

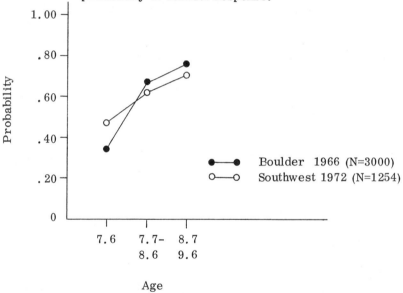

Due to sampling restrictions of the former sample, it is possible to plot only the scores for three age groups, 7 years 6 months and younger, 7 years 7 months to 8 years 6 months, and 8 years 7 months to 9 years 6 months. However, as may be seen, the groups generate approximately the same configuration, suggesting very similar performance and, more importantly, developmental levels for the two groups.

4.7 Summary. On the basis of these analyses then, it must be said that despite regionally related differences between the sites and differences in sample selection, there are no meaningful site differences in performance. Furthermore, with respect to sex, it must be said that our data do not provide adequate evidence to assume that there are sex differences and field dependence differences on the neo-Piagetian measures. Finally, and perhaps most importantly, the data indicate that there are no ethnic group differences on the neo-Piagetian developmental measures.

CHAPTER 5

DISCUSSION

The preceding data, though numerous, are organized around five issues. These are: the psychometric properties of the group neo-Piagetian measures, the developmental properties of these measures, the performance of the sample as a whole on the developmental measures, the performance of each site sample on developmental and standardized measures, and a comparison of sites. It would be helpful if at this point these issues were enumerated and discussed before any attempts are made to integrate them into a larger body of thought. Before covering these issues, however, it is important to bear in mind that this study is a field study subject to the shortcomings inherent in field research. In general, there was not the level of control over variables that would seem to be desirable. For example, achievement tests were different at each site, which precluded any comparison of achievement levels across sites. A widespread result of lack of control over variables was a limited range of some major variables, i.e. socioeconomic status (SES), ethnicity, and capacity. In a more rigorous study perhaps some of the inferences we have been forced to make would not be necessary as there would be pertinent data available.

Studies are needed wherein SES, ethnicity, language facility, sociocultural factors, and capacity are rigorously defined and data collected at a number of different sites. Hopefully, this would enable researchers to examine the relative importance of these factors in contributing to cognitive development and school performance, and the relationship between the two. Procedures could then be directed toward modifying circumstances over which we have some degree of control, such as curriculum design.

Studies could employ multiple regression techniques (Tatsuoka 1969) in order to establish the relative importance of various SES, linguistic, and sociocultural variables for school performance of different ethnic groups. In this way, it would be possible to determine whether the same set of variables usually used to predict success for the majority Anglo-American children applied to other groups with equal predictive validity. Furthermore, more knowledge would be gained about successful performance of Anglo-American children. The present data suggest that the regression equation describing Mexican-American children would be different from that of the majority middle class in that development, as measured by De Avila's and Pascual-Leone's neo-Piagetian measures, would be of less importance whereas social factors represented in the tests and curriculum would be of greater importance. Given these concerns and limitations, and our hopes for future study, a number of points remain both appropriate and important.

5.1 Psychometric properties. Of initial concern were the psychometric properties of the group neo-Piagetian measures. These four measures--the CCS, the WLT, the FIT, and the ST--were subjected to various psychometric analyses. Each scale (and subscale when appropriate) was examined for reliability and internal consistency by age group and for the total sample. The following indices of reliability and internal consistency were used: KR-20, Cronbach's alpha, part/whole correlations, and W. A. Scott's homogeneity ratio (H.R.). Factor analyses were also employed where appropriate. The results of the analyses for the CCS, WLT, and FIT measures were of sufficient order to warrant their acceptance as measurement devices. The current version of the ST is not acceptable and requires revision.

5.2 Developmental properties. The second issue considered was the developmental properties of these four instruments. Do these measures, in fact, reflect developmental increments as age increases? First, total scores on all four instruments were correlated with chronological age. All of them were significantly correlated with age. The ST, however, had the least degree of relationship with age. Second, all of the subscales were intercorrelated and also correlated with chronological age. All of these correlations except two were statistically significant. Examining the pattern of correlations indicates that CCS/weight tends to correlate less well with other subscales and with age than any other test (this is perhaps due to overall low performance on it, as would be expected from Piagetian theory). Another method of examining the developmental properties of these measures was to plot probability of a correct response by scales (and subscales where appropriate) across age. If these measures were developmentally sound, they would exhibit a linear relationship between age and performance. The CCS subscales do, in fact, yield such a configuration. Also, the rank order of difficulty of the items is consistent with Piaget's functional analysis of the different conservation tasks.

The WLT subscales were also plotted. The performance represents a linear relationship between age and performance. In addition, the rank order of difficulty of the items is consistent with Pascual-Leone's analysis of them.

The total scores on the CCS, WLT, FIT, and ST were also plotted. Except for the ST, all of these exhibit developmental progression and an expected level of performance. The graph of the ST indicates that there is not much of an increment in performance across age and that the overall level of performance is quite low. It is interesting to note that the configuration of the CCS and the FIT are quite close.

In summary, then, of the first two issues of concern, it may be said that three of the four developmental neo-Piagetian measures were shown to be both psychometrically viable and developmentally sound.

5.3 Cognitive-developmental level of four-state sample. The third issue is the performance of the entire sample on the neo-Piagetian measures in relation to predictions generated by Piagetian theory of cognitive development. Potentially a theoretical issue only, in current times the issue of the performance of Spanish-American children has found itself in the political arena due to civil rights efforts and recent well-publicized articles by Jensen, Shockley, and others. Thus, the performance of this basically Mexican-American sample has great political and social import. Their performance was not particularly divergent from the performance score in other research using the same concepts, or from the expected age of acquisition reported in Piaget's work.

5.4 Performance on each site. The fourth major concern of this investigation was the performance of each of the four sites individually on both the developmental neo-Piagetian measures and on the commercial standardized tests.

5.4.1 New Mexico. The first site to be examined proved to be very interesting. While performance by grade on both sets of measures was in no way unexpected or remarkable, examination by sex and ethnicity yielded a number of differences of potentially great importance. The sex differences are not consistent or systematic, but interesting. Examining the total sample, males perform at more advanced cognitive levels than females on the developmental measures in five of twelve cases, including total scores on the CCS, WLT, and FIT. In contrast, there are no sex differences on the Otis-Lennon. On the achievement measure--the CTBS--significant main effects of sex indicate that females perform better than males in language skills areas in grades two and three only. These findings would imply a greater need for the establishment of sex-based norms than for the ethnicity-based norms which have been currently suggested by a large number of test publishers (see De Avila and Havassy 1973) for the problems inherent in such an approach).

The analyses of performance by ethnicity yielded additional findings of interest. First, while there are no ethnic group differences on the developmental neo-Piagetian measures, there are consistent significant ethnic group differences on the Otis-Lennon for every grade. All of them are in the same direction: Anglo-American children perform significantly better than the Mexican-American children. Viewing performance on the achievement test, the CTBS, adds another dimension to ethnic differences. CTBS ethnic differences emerge in special cases only. In grade one, Anglo-American children do better on the aural comprehension scale. In grades two and three there is a sex-ethnicity interaction on the vocabulary scale only, with Anglo-American females scoring the highest, followed by Mexican-American females, followed by Mexican-American males, with Anglo-American males scoring the lowest.

In grades four, five, and six there are sex-ethnicity interactions, all of them replicating a single pattern. The pattern consists of Anglo-American males scoring the highest, with the two female groups scoring the next highest--being very close together on performance--and the Mexican-American male being clearly the poorest performer. This pattern is found on the following scales of the CTBS: arithmetic concepts, arithmetic application, study skills, and the total CTBS score.

5.4.2 Colorado. The Colorado site results were in no way unusual. Performance was generally average, with some minor deviations from average performance in some of the grades. Only sex differences could be examined in this sample. On the neo-Piagetian measures there were few sex differences. On the CCS and WLT total scores, males performed at more advanced levels than females. There were minor sex differences on the CTMM in each grade, but none on the achievement measure.

5.4.3 Texas. Texas data were difficult to integrate and interpret. This was the case because the testing was incomplete except for the neo-Piagetian measures; therefore, test results did not provide much information. Grades one through three received no measure of capacity and the achievement measure administered to grades one through six assessed reading achievement only. Furthermore, the data exist in raw score form only (no norms are provided by the

publishers of the Inter-American Series), thus making any sort of
data interpretation impossible. The high number of children overage
for grade at this site further hampers interpretation of data. The
only performance differences according to sex were found in the neo-
Piagetian measures, where seven of the twelve comparisons yielded
sex differences in favor of males, including total scores on the CCS,
WLT, and FIT. In fact, there were more sex differences on the
developmental measures at this site than at any other site.

5.4.4 California. The data obtained at the California site were
also inconclusive except for the developmental data, which showed
that these children have reached levels of cognitive development
appropriate for their chronological age despite their being a part of
the migrant stream and not receiving the benefits of a systematic
curriculum in a language understood by them. When examined for
sex differences the developmental data indicated few differences--
the least of all the sites--and a high level of performance. On the
PPVT, there tended to be low scores but no sex differences.

5.5 Differences between sites. The fifth issue was the comparative performance of each site on the developmental neo-Piagetian
measures. While the ANOVAs showed a statistically significant site
effect, there were no meaningful site differences in performance on
the neo-Piagetian measures. This means that the developmental
levels of the different children tested were virtually the same. It
should be noted that the total population represented a fairly narrow
range of the SES continuum. It should not be inferred that these
results indicate that if children from extreme SES groups were compared, there would be no differences. In fact, the home environments
of the very rich and the very poor are sufficiently different to imply
that there would be a difference in development. The fact nevertheless
remains that, according to the present findings, children from fairly
diverse cultural and linguistic backgrounds did not differ in development.

Given this overview of results it becomes important to step back
from these data and view them in a more global or general manner so
that their implications for psychological theory and for larger con-
temporary social and political issues may become apparent. The
authors would like to make the following points with respect to the
present body of data.

This study involves, as a primary goal, an attempt to use measures
derived from Piagetian theory of cognitive development to assess the
highest level of intellectual functioning possessed by different age
groups within the Mexican-American population. Due to problems
associated with using standardized tests with Spanish-language

background children (see De Avila and Havassy 1973), the procedures employed in the present research are geared toward the facilitation of performance through linguistic and conceptual pretraining for each neo-Piagetian test and through the modified use of a 'controlled repertoire' paradigm. In this approach standardized item content is used, while the test instructions vary according to the needs of the child. It stands in contrast to the traditional standardized procedures where concern is given to the standardization of test instructions and of wording of test items.

The findings of the present research reveal that when these methods and procedures are employed, Mexican-American children perform at cognitive levels appropriate for their chronological age. Even though there is a statistically significant variation of performance across sites, all performance is well within the normal range of appropriate level of cognitive functioning. A related and equally important finding of this research is that it failed to find differences in the level of cognitive developmental performance between Anglo- and Mexican-American children. The data show the same developmental curves for both ethnic groups. These findings are supportive of Piagetian theory. From these findings the authors conclude that Mexican-American children develop cognitively the same as, and at basically the same rate as, Anglo-American children. It should be noted that this position is contrary to that espoused by Jensen (1971).

Given our findings and conclusions, it is important to relate the current sample's performance on the neo-Piagetian measures to ethnic differences on capacity and achievement tests which favor Anglo-American children, and to the general failure of Mexican-American children to achieve in schools. The failure to achieve in schools, to perform well on capacity and achievement measures, and the differences between ethnic groups, must be attributed to reasons other than the alleged cognitive inability of the Mexican-American child, since our data show that there is no difference between Mexican- and Anglo-American children. Some of the reasons, we believe, lie in the standardized tests and curriculum which are used throughout the schools.

5.6 Commerical standardized tests of capacity and achievement. The difference in performance of Mexican-American children on the neo-Piagetian measures where they perform at levels as cognitively complex as their Anglo-American counterparts, and on the standardized tests of capacity and achievement where they perform less ably than these counterparts, is attributed in part to the underlying biases of these standardized tests. It is believed that the neo-Piagetian measures used with the modified controlled repertoire procedure are identifying the 'false negatives' of traditional commercial standardized tests, i. e. children who have been incorrectly represented as having low ability and capacity to achieve. These commercial tests assume a common uniform cultural experience, as well as verbal and/or written facility with the English language. They are accurate measuring devices when the background of the student matches the one inherent in the test. Cultural and linguistic differences, as they affect capacity and achievement tests, are an obvious problem and have been acknowledged as such in the psychological literature (see, for example, Cronbach 1960; McClelland 1973). That the problem is accepted by the testing industry is reflected in the recent attempts at translations of tests and the creation of 'Spanish-speaking' norms. That these attempts are misguided and insufficient has been argued elsewhere by the authors (De Avila and Havassy 1973). The main point here is that Mexican-American children, to the extent they do not partake of the mainstream culture, perform poorly on standardized commercial tests simply because these tests are culturally and linguistically biased.

5. 7 School curriculum. The other factor to which the authors attribute the poor performance of Mexican-American children on achievement tests is that of the curriculum with which they are presented in the schools. The present data suggest that populations of Mexican- and Anglo-American children who are equal with respect to cognitive developmental level (according to Piagetian theory) will not be equal in school-related achievement. This condition implies that cognitive development is not in itself a sufficient factor to engender a level of school achievement in Mexican-American children equal to that of Anglo-American children. The conclusion to be drawn is that the curriculum approach taken with Mexican-American children must be questioned, examined, and revised. It would appear that the curriculum and teacher-student relations are also as biased as the capacity and achievement tests with regard to language and culture.

All of these critical remarks lead us to conjecture about the outcome under the most benign circumstances possible. It is believed that under such conditions, where curriculum meets the educational needs of all children and tests are not biased, there would be a congruence between the neo-Piagetian and standardized measures. Lack of congruence between the two sets of measures, which is generally due to poor performance on standardized measures, only points to problems in environmental circumstances, including the schools and curriculum. Children are not responsible for such circumstances and should not be penalized for them.

5. 8 Summary. A field study involving approximately 1, 300 Mexican-American and Anglo-American children from four

southwestern states was conducted. The sample was tested using standardized tests of school achievement, IQ, and four Piagetian-derived measures. The goals of the research were as follows: first, to test the interrelations among the four neo-Piagetian measures in a Mexican-American sample which varied in terms of geography and SES; second, to examine the psychometric properties of these neo-Piagetian measures; third, to examine the relation between developmental level as assessed by the neo-Piagetian procedures, and IQ as assessed by standardized measures; fourth, to examine the extent of field-independence as measured by Pascual-Leone's Water Level Task; and fifth, to examine site and sex differences in performance on the tests.

The most important results of this research have shown the following.

(1) Three of the four neo-Piagetian measures (Cartoon Conservation Scales, Water Level Task, Figural Intersections Test) are psychometrically sound; they possess high reliability, homogeneity, and validity.

(2) These measures exhibit a developmental progression of performance scores across age in accordance with Piaget's theory of cognitive development.

(3) The performance of the predominantly Mexican-American sample is developmentally appropriate and well within the limits of expected levels of cognitive development, given chronological ages.

(4) There are no meaningful differences between the sexes on the four neo-Piagetian measures.

(5) There are no meaningful differences in performance between the four geographic locations where the data were collected. Site differences, when they occur, tended to be for the three youngest age groups, oldest age of 9 years, 6 months.

(6) A comparison of the performance of children taking the tests in English, Spanish, or bilingually, revealed no appreciable differences; differences in cognitive development as measured by the Piagetian tests could not be attributed to differences in language. This finding stands in contrast to earlier work which has suggested that bilingualism is an impediment to cognitive development.

(7) At the New Mexico location, the only place where ethnic group comparisons could be made, there were no ethnic group differences on the four neo-Piagetian measures. In contrast, there were consistent ethnic group differences on the capacity measure (Otis-Lennon Mental Abilities Test) and on the achievement measure (Comprehensive Test of Basic Skills). The direction of these differences was always in favor of Anglo-American children.

These results have several implications for future research. First, as the present study is a field study, a study is needed where there is greater control over some of the independent variables. Studies are required where the samples are stratified in terms of SES, ethnicity, sex, and capacity, and where the extreme groups of these variables are represented. Furthermore, data should be gathered on degree of assimilation and on language dominance. With such controls, the nature of the relationship between neo-Piagetian measures and traditional measures of capacity and achievement, and the influence of the former variables on the relationship, could be assessed with greater precision.

Second, the results of this study indicate that the relationship between cognitive development and school achievement, especially of minority children, must be more closely examined. Our data suggest that populations of Mexican-American and Anglo-American children who are equal with respect to cognitive development (according to Piagetian theory) will not be equal in school-related achievement. This finding implies that cognitive development in Mexican-American children, and perhaps other children, is not itself a sufficient condition to engender a level of school achievement equal to that of Anglo-American middle-class children.

The social and educational implications of our findings are as follows: First, the failure to find differences between Anglo- and Mexican-American children on the neo-Piagetian measures leads us to adopt the position that Mexican-American children develop cognitively the same as, and at basically the same rate as Anglo-American children. These results are contrary to the position espoused by Jensen (1971), who suggests that Mexican-American children cannot perform certain cognitive activities that Anglo-American children can because of genetic endowment.

Second, the failure of Mexican-American children to achieve in schools and to perform well on capacity and achievement measures must be attributed to reasons other than the alleged cognitive inability of the Mexican-American child since our data show no inability. Some of these reasons for failure lie in traditional tests and in curriculum used throughout the schools. The materials, language, and situational context utilized both in testing and in curriculum are culturally biased in favor of the Anglo-American middle-class culture and (all) children who do not share that culture are at a disadvantage in such situations.

REFERENCES

Adams, J. A. 1967. Human memory. New York, McGraw Hill.

Binet, Alfred. 1908. Les idées modernes sur les enfants. Paris, Ernest Flamarion.

Brown, Roger. 1965. Social psychology. New York, The Free Press.

Cronbach, L. J. 1960. Essentials of psychological testing, 2nd ed. New York, Harper and Brothers.

De Avila, E. A. and J. Struthers. 1967. Development of a group measure to assess the extent of prelogical and precausal thinking in primary school age children. Paper presented to National Science Teachers' Association Convention, Detroit.

De Avila, E. A., J. A. Struthers, and D. L. Randall. 1969. A group measure of the Piagetian concepts of conservation and ego-centricity. Canadian Journal of Behavioural Science 1(4). 263-272.

De Avila, E. A. and J. M. Phyphers. 1968. Boulder looks at Title I children. Denver, Colorado Department of Education.

De Avila, E. A. 1971. Children's transformation of visual information according to nonverbal syntactical rules. Doctoral thesis, York University. In preparation.

De Avila, E. A. and B. Havassy. 1973. Some critical notes on using IQ tests for minority children: A Piagetian-based information system as an alternative and results of a field study. Paper presented at Conference of National Task Force de la Raza, UCLA, July.

Dodwell, P. C. 1961. Children's understanding of number concepts: Characteristics of an individual and of a group test. Canadian Journal of Psychology 15. 29-36.

Elkind, D. 1970. Conceptions of intelligence. Harvard Review.

Goodnow, Jacqueline J. 1963. A test of milieu effects with some of Piaget's tasks. Air Force contract AF 49(638)-682.

89

Harker, W. A. 1960. Children's number concepts: Ordination and coordination. Unpublished Master's thesis. Douglas Library, Queen's University, Kingston, Ontario.

Hays, W. L. 1963. Statistics for psychologists. New York, Holt, Rinehart, Winston.

Hunt, J. M. 1961. Intelligence and experience. New York, Ronald Press Company.

Jensen, A. R. 1971a. Do schools cheat minority children? Educational Research 14.3-28.

_____. 1971b. A two factor theory of mental retardation. Paper presented at the 4th International Congress of Human Genetics, Paris.

Lesser, G. S., G. Fifer, and B. H. Clark. 1965. Mental abilities of children of different social classes and cultural groups. Monographs of the Society for Research Child Development, No. 102.

McClelland, D. 1973. Testing for competence rather than for intelligence. American Psychologist 28.1-14.

Mercer, J. 1971. The meaning of mental retardation. In: The mentally retarded child and his family: A multidisciplinary handbook. Ed. by R. Koch and J. Dobson. New York, Brunner and Hazel.

Merselstein, E. 1968. The impact of school attendance on Piaget's conservation tasks. Cited in D. C. Randall, unpublished doctoral dissertation. University of Colorado.

Newman-Keuls. 1962. Method for ad hoc cell comparisons. Cited in B. J. Winer, Statistical principles in experimental design. New York, McGraw-Hill.

Pascual-Leone, J. and E. A. De Avila. 1971. Cognitive development and learning from a neo-Piagetian constructive point of view. Paper read at University of Western Ontario Colloquium Series, January.

Pascual-Leone, J. 1970. A mathematical model for the transition rule in Piaget's developmental stages. Acta Psychologia 32.301-45.

Pascual-Leone, J. and G. Parkinson. 1969. The development of cognitive information, Studies I and II. Research reports R691 and R706. York University.

Pascual-Leone, J. and June Smith. 1968. The encoding and decoding of symbols by children: A new experimental paradigm and a neo-Piagetian model. Journal of Experimental Child Psychology 8.328-55.

Phillips, J. L. 1969. The origins of intellect. San Francisco, Freeman and Co.

Piaget, J. 1952. The origins and intelligence in children. New York, International University Press.

Piaget, J. and B. Inhelder. 1948. La représentation de l'espace chez l'enfant. Paris, P.U.F. English translation: The child's conception of space. London, Routledge and Kegan Paul.

Ramirez, M., III. 1972. Cognitive styles: Cultural democracy in education. Social Science Quarterly.

Saarni, C. I. 1973. Piagetian operations and field independence as factors in children's problem-solving performance. Child Development 44. 338-345.

Sanchez, George I. 1932. Group differences and Spanish-speaking children: A critical review. Journal of Applied Psychology 549-558.

Scheffe, H. A. 1953. A method for judging all possible contrasts in the analysis of variance. Biometrica 40. 87-104.

Scott, W. A. 1960. Measures to test homogeneity. Educational and Psychological Measurement 20. 751-757.

Tatsuoka, Maurice M. 1969. Selected topics in advanced statistics. No. 5. Illinois, The Institute for Personality and Ability Testing.

Wallach, M. A. 1963. Research on children's thinking. In: National Society for the Study of Education, 62nd yearbook, Child psychology. Chicago, University of Chicago Press.

Witkin, K. A., R. B. Dyk, H. F. Faterson, D. R. Goodenough, and S. A. Karp. 1962. Psychological differentiation: Studies of development. New York, Wiley.